Talk That Teaches

Teaching Practices That Work

Diane Lapp and Douglas Fisher, Series Editors
www.guilford.com/TPTW

Designed specifically for busy teachers who value evidence-based instructional practices, books in this series offer ready-to-implement strategies and tools to promote student engagement, improve teaching and learning across the curriculum, and support the academic growth of all students in our increasingly diverse schools. Written by expert authors with extensive experience in "real-time" classrooms, each concise and accessible volume provides useful explanations and examples to guide instruction, as well as step-by-step methods and reproducible materials, all in a convenient large-size format for ease of photocopying. Recent titles have Web pages where purchasers can download and print the reproducible materials.

Talk That Teaches

Using Strategic Talk to Help Students Achieve the Common Core

Jeanne R. Paratore
Dana A. Robertson

Series Editors' Note by
Diane Lapp and Douglas Fisher

THE GUILFORD PRESS
New York   London

© 2013 The Guilford Press
A Division of Guilford Publications, Inc.
72 Spring Street, New York, NY 10012
www.guilford.com

Printed in the United States of America

This book is printed on acid-free paper.

Last digit is print number: 9   8   7   6   5   4   3   2   1

Library of Congress Cataloging-in-Publication Data is available from the Publisher

ISBN 978-1-4625-1042-9

About the Authors

Jeanne R. Paratore, EdD, is Professor of Education and Coordinator of the Reading Education and Literacy and Language Education Programs at Boston University. She is a former classroom teacher, reading specialist, and Title I director. Dr. Paratore was inducted into the Reading Hall of Fame in 2011 and is a recipient of the New England Reading Association's Lifetime Achievement Award and the International Reading Association's Celebrate Literacy Award. She has conducted research and published widely on issues related to family literacy, classroom grouping practices, and interventions for struggling readers. She is also a coauthor of one of the nation's leading reading programs, Reading Street.

Dana A. Robertson, EdD, is Assistant Professor of Elementary and Early Childhood Education at the University of Wyoming. He is a former classroom teacher, reading specialist, and literacy coach. Dr. Robertson was a featured teacher in the video series *Teaching Reading, 3–5*, produced by WGBH Television and the Annenberg Foundation. His research and publications focus on teacher talk, comprehension strategies instruction, and teacher professional development.

Series Editors' Note

As our schools continue to grow in linguistic, cultural, and socioeconomic diversity, educators are committed to implementing instruction that supports individual and collective growth within their classrooms. In tandem with teacher commitment, schools recognize the need to support teacher collaboration on issues related to implementing, evaluating, and expanding instruction to ensure that all students will one day graduate from high school with the skills needed to succeed in the workforce. Through our work with teachers across the country, we've become aware of the need for books that can be used to support professional collaboration by grade level and subject area. With these teachers' questions in mind, we decided that a series of books was needed that modeled "real-time" teaching and learning within classroom instruction. Thus the series *Teaching Practices That Work* was born.

Books in this series are distinguished by offering instructional examples that have been studied and refined within authentic classroom settings. Each book is written by one or more educators who are well connected to everyday classroom instruction. Because the series editors are themselves classroom teachers as well as professors, each instructional suggestion has been closely scrutinized for its validity.

In *Talk That Teaches: Using Strategic Talk to Help Students Achieve the Common Core*, Jeanne R. Paratore and Dana A. Robertson open by inviting readers into a conference room to discuss with colleagues how to best support learning for all students, especially those who struggle with literacy practices. The first task they pose is to list questions you would expect such a group to ask. If you are like the teachers they actually invited to do this task, none of your resulting questions would address the need for *teacher talk* or how to make your own talk more instructionally meaningful. Having set the stage, the authors then guide us to understand that students must use their language, and what they know about language, to constantly learn increasingly difficult concepts. Paratore and Robertson challenge teachers to lessen the struggle that students have with language by systematically assessing each student's language knowledge and then designing instruction that builds from a base of real knowledge about the learner. The examples they offer clarify the differences among *goal-setting talk, explanatory talk,* and *feedback talk,* while also scaffolding our understanding of the purposeful instruction that supports each. Their detailed lesson examples illustrate how to employ very meaningful teacher talk to help students build their vocabulary, comprehension, and writing skills across grade levels and disciplines.

The book's systematic approach to lesson design and its numerous reproducible forms help to support easy implementation of the lessons you may design to accomplish similar standards. Each lesson example remains true to the major goals of the text, which are, first, to help teachers understand the powerful relationship between teacher and student talk and learning, and, second, to make instructional language interactions so well focused that students' oral language learning continues to develop. As educators have reported for decades, students who experience academic success have high levels of meaningful vocabulary knowledge, and their increasing oral competence supports their mastering of reading and writing skills. This valuable book helps to make the possibility of language expansion and consequent literacy success available to every student.

We invite you into the "real-time" teaching offered in this book and hope you'll find this series useful as you validate and expand your teaching repertoire. And if you have an idea for a book, please contact us!

DIANE LAPP
DOUGLAS FISHER

• •

Introduction

Pretend, for a moment, that you are sitting in a conference room with a group of teachers and administrators. The purpose of the meeting is to discuss ways to improve instruction so that children who are struggling in reading and writing have increased opportunities to learn. Imagine the conversation—what recommendations do you suppose you would hear? In recent weeks, we have posed this question a number of times to teachers in a range of schools and communities. We found a clear pattern in responses: Some focused on meeting Common Core State Standards (CCSS; National Governors Association Center for Best Practices & Council of Chief State School Officers, 2010), including questions about text complexity ("Our kids can't read on grade level—we can't use complex text with them") and about "close reading" ("I don't think I really know what 'close' reading is or the best way to teach it"). Others focused on issues that have perplexed teachers of reading for many years, including appropriateness of *text levels* ("We need to think about the texts children are reading—children need texts matched to their reading levels"); *curriculum needs* ("We need a new reading program—the program we have is old and does not have interesting selections"); *time* ("We need more time to teach reading; we don't have time to meet all of our groups every day"); *specialized support* ("We can't meet the range of needs of all the students in our classrooms; we need a reading teacher to take the kids who need extra help"); and *parental support* ("We need to get parents to read with children at home; we won't be able to improve their reading if they never read at home").

These are, of course, all factors that contribute to children's opportunities to learn. But notice what is missing from this list. We did not hear a single mention of the need to harness *teacher talk* as a resource in improving children's opportunities to learn. Although we were not surprised by this omission, we were concerned by it. Despite decades of compelling theory and research on the importance of talk (e.g., Cazden, 2001; Boyd & Galda, 2011), it has yet to take a central place as a curriculum resource in most classrooms. Planful and strategic teacher talk provides a powerful resource to meet CCSS in general, and, in particular, the demand that students articulate, justify, and defend their understanding and interpretation of text both orally and in writing. That said, appropriate use of teacher talk requires teachers to engage in a bit of a balancing act: They are encouraged to guide students to think critically about texts by selecting and ordering questions such that "they bootstrap onto each other and promote deep thinking and substantive engagement with the text" (Coleman & Pimentel, 2012, p. 9). But they are also reminded not to frame instruction in ways that "preempt or replace the text by translating its contents for teachers or tell students what they are going to learn in advance of reading the text" (Coleman & Pimentel, 2012, p. 8). For some, the differences and distinctions between these ideas might be difficult to discern. Are there particular talk "stems" or strategies that are more productive in "bootstrapping" students' text understanding and interpretation and less likely to simply guide students to adopt the teachers' point of view? Our purpose in this book is to explore the question of how teacher talk can best be used to support students' development as capable readers and critical thinkers. We do so by addressing two central ideas:

1 *Why* the importance of teacher talk should be elevated.

2 *How* teachers can refine their talk to engage their students in thoughtful and productive reading and writing.

Why Should We Pay Attention to Teacher Talk?

When we think about the kinds of readers and writers we want our students to be—the literate lives we want them to lead—the words that immediately come to mind are *purposeful*, *thoughtful*, and *engaged*. We want our students to use their literacy skills purposefully both in and out of school—to learn more about their world, to solve everyday problems, to act on their citizenry, and to be entertained. Whatever the reading purpose, we want our students to thoughtfully and deliberately adjust their focus and strategy use to attain their learning goals. We also want them to know that engaging in discussion with others helps deepen their understanding of new concepts and may also heighten their enjoyment and motivation to read and write; and we want them to understand that writing both deepens and sustains understanding and can serve as a vehicle for sharing their thinking with others.

Teachers' planful and strategic use of talk is a powerful instructional resource in helping students to become purposeful, thoughtful, and engaged readers and writers. Evidence tells us that skillful teacher talk:

- Supports higher levels of student engagement and motivation (Johnston, Ivey, & Faulkner, 2011; Wells, 2001).
- Supports the development of problem-solving strategies (Gaskins, Anderson, Pressley, Cunicelli, & Saltow, 1993; Johnston, 2012).

◆ Supports the development of self-concept as a capable learner (Johnston, 2012).

◆ Encourages elaborated student thinking (Frey & Fisher, 2010; Johnston, 2012).

◆ Results in growth in student understanding (Mercer, Wegerif, & Dawes, 1999; Wolf, Crosson, & Resnick, 2006).

However, gaining masterful control of effective instructional talk is not an easy task. When writing about her own journey in understanding and using more skillful teacher talk, Denton (2007) aptly noted that "the appearance of spontaneity and intuitiveness was a byproduct of repeated doing, reflecting, adjusting, doing again, reflecting" (p. 5).

Skillful teachers flexibly and adaptively employ a range of strategic talk moves to meet the diverse needs of learners. They use talk to help their students establish goals for their learning, to explain and model strategic actions to prompt students to construct meaning and to deepen and evaluate their thinking, and to provide continual explicit feedback that informs students of their progress toward meeting their goals. Teachers who carefully and purposefully choose their words help students acquire identities as individuals who skillfully use reading and writing to get things done in the real world. Teachers who leverage talk as a curriculum resource are, as Johnston (2012) notes, akin to accomplished jazz musicians, responding, adapting, and changing moment to moment, based on what they see and hear:

> Teaching is planned opportunism. We have an idea of what we want to teach children, and we plan ways to make that learning possible. When we put our plans into action, children offer us opportunities to say something, or not, and the choices we make affect what happens next. Teaching requires constant improvisation. It is jazz. (p. 4)

But what are the particular types of talk that seem to advance students' understanding, learning, and self-direction? In the next section we present three general "talk types" that seem to make a difference in students' reading and writing success.

What Types of Talk Do We Need?

As we plan and implement our instruction, we focus on three types of talk: *Goal-setting talk* develops students' explicit awareness of reading and writing goals and of ways to set them for themselves; *explanatory talk* develops students' awareness, understanding, and ability to use strategies; and *feedback talk* audits (i.e., helps students know how they are doing) and informs (i.e., details the steps or procedures that will help the student maintain a successful performance or improve a less successful performance) (Wiggins, 1993).

Goal-Setting Talk

Goal-setting talk focuses on developing an understanding of each lesson's learning goals and of the connection between the goals and children's lives both inside and outside of school. Although this definition sounds relatively straightforward, such a focus is not always plainly evident in classrooms. Sometimes instruction is centered on the skill or the content of the task, rather than on the overall knowledge or outcome that is likely to result from task completion. For example, we recently met with a small group of teachers who were planning to teach a unit on reading biographies. We asked why they were planning this unit—what was the learning goal that they wanted children to achieve? Teachers immediately responded that reading biography was one of the expectations included in the state's instructional framework. We acknowledged this point, but pressed further: Why, we asked, is reading biography worthy of inclusion in the state's literacy framework? Why might one read a biography outside of school? What prompted *them*, as able readers, to choose to read about the lives of others?

After much hesitation, teachers began to consider and explain their own reading habits. One chose to read about individuals who might inspire, another chose to read about individuals who might help understand a context or culture different from her own, yet another chose to read about individuals from a certain historical period. As we talked, it became evident that in their own reading, they sought texts that helped them deepen their knowledge about a person or place or time that was of particular interest to them—that they were, in fact, choosing texts on the basis of information (knowledge) they wanted to acquire about their world. We talked a bit about the relationship between their own motivation and engagement, their *knowledge goals* (i.e., what they wanted to know more about), and their reading choices. We shared evidence of the relationship between students' explicit knowledge goals and increased motivation and engagement (Guthrie & Humineck, 2004), and we discussed implications for planning lessons with their students. We encouraged teachers to consider the difference between literacy goals (developing skills and strategies to improve reading/writing proficiency) and knowledge goals (acquiring new concepts and understandings about the world). We emphasized that for students to acquire and sustain interest and motivation in reading and writing both in and out of school, they must see that reading and writing serve as vehicles for acquiring and sharing new and important information about their world. Teachers who routinely engage in goal-setting talk—talk that focuses both on why (knowledge goals) and how (literacy goals) students might read texts—contribute to the development of a purposeful, strategic, and engaged disposition in their students toward reading and writing.

Explanatory Talk

To accomplish their goals, skilled readers and writers flexibly employ strategies that facilitate their understanding of texts they read and their ability to convey meaning through their writing. Skillful teachers use *explanatory talk* that thoroughly and thoughtfully details each level of strategy knowledge (Paris, Lipson, & Wixson, 1994). That is, they identify *what* strategies students should use (declarative knowledge); they explain *how* a strategy is enacted during reading or writing (procedural knowledge); and they explain when or why a particular strategy is helpful in meeting their learning goals (conditional knowledge). Further, teachers model the use of the strategy, talking aloud to make their own thinking "visible" for students, and they share personal experiences with using the strategy.

After modeling, effective teachers guide students in applying strategies, supporting their development of conceptual understandings and deepening the meaning of the texts they are reading and creating, all under the watchful eyes of the teachers. Teacher talk that guides students' strategy use incorporates several key characteristics (Frey & Fisher, 2010; Johnston et al., 2011). Such talk:

- Focuses on open-ended, "real" questions (i.e., not questions to which the teacher already knows the answer).
- Elaborates or clarifies students' thinking.
- Prompts students to elaborate or clarify thinking, provide evidence for thinking, and connect ideas.
- Prompts students to engage in strategic actions.
- Cues students to focus their attention on useful resources (e.g., a classroom anchor chart) or on particular aspects of the text (e.g., a particular page or overarching text structure) that will support strategy use or conceptual understanding.
- Explains and models strategic actions when students demonstrate the need for more explicit guidance.

Explanatory talk provides students with apprenticed practice in reading and writing strategically, while also providing teachers with multiple opportunities to formatively assess students' understanding. Moreover, engaging students in guided practice gives them the opportunity to collaborate with their classmates in co-constructing understandings, while also conveying the message to students that they are all capable learners and are all expected to participate. Guided practice further develops students' procedural and conditional strategy knowledge by cueing them to appropriate times to engage in strategic actions and providing the right amount of scaffolding for them to successfully employ strategic actions (Duffy, 2009). Furthermore, it provides a rich context for developing conceptual understanding and content knowledge, and thus facilitates students' acquisition of higher-order, critical thinking skills (Beck, McKeown, & Kucan, 2008).

Strategy instruction will most likely be transferred to a new context when the lesson in which it is taught and practiced is purposeful and meaningful (Calkins, 2003, 2006; Johnston, 2004). Moreover, when planning and implementing strategy instruction, effective teachers keep "the main thing the main thing" (Duffy, 2009, p. 3); that is, they teach and maintain strategy knowledge as a means to an end (i.e., developing a clear and coherent understanding of text) rather than as an end itself (e.g., being able to recite the main idea).

Skillful explanatory talk accomplishes two purposes: (1) It defines a strategy, and (2) it develops awareness and understanding of how and when to use the strategy. As such, it prepares students to engage in strategy use not only when they are told to do so, but also to self-initiate strategy use in response to particular reading and writing demands (Johnston et al., 2011).

Feedback Talk

Feedback talk *audits*—it tells students how they are doing; and it *informs*—it details the steps or procedures that will help students maintain a successful performance or improve a less successful one (Wiggins, 1993). Efficacious feedback focuses students' attention on strategic actions (e.g., "I noticed that when you were uncertain, you reread the page—that's a great strategy for clarifying your understanding"), rather than on global praise (e.g., "Excellent job!") (Johnston, 2004, 2012). The practice of combining an evaluative comment with an explicit description of the process or strategy that was (or could be) helpful promotes students' agency and their sense that they can control or manage their own learning (Johnston et al., 2011).

Feedback talk may sometimes overlap with explanatory talk, especially when feedback is intended to clarify a misconception. For example:

> "I noticed that you drew a quick conclusion about the character after reading the first episode. But in the second episode, the character acts a bit differently. Sometimes an author creates a character who has many different moods or traits, and to really understand what's happening, we have to keep an open mind about the sort of person the character is. So, let's go back and reread the second episode, and think about the new information the author tells us about the character and see if it helps you understand what happened next."

In this example, the teacher's feedback is both evaluative— "you drew a quick conclusion"—and explanatory, describing what the student might do to clarify and deepen understanding. For students to routinely and successfully engage in strategic actions, we need to provide explicit and timely feedback in a situated context—that is, a context in which the strategy can be readily applied. As such, *feedback talk* is often intertwined with explanatory talk, and it often occurs within the context of guided practice.

Talking the Talk

Although it may sound simple to incorporate these types of talk into instruction, effective use of these talk moves is complex. Skillful teachers understand how to successfully orchestrate these talk moves "on the run" to address the varied learning needs of their students. In the sections that follow, we consider three literacy domains: vocabulary, comprehension, and writing. For each, we describe strategies that have been documented as beneficial for students' reading success, and we explain what each strategy is and why it is important. Next, we describe how to teach the strategy, and we provide a detailed lesson plan as an example. Then, as a way to eavesdrop on the lesson and "hear the talk" in action, we provide a transcript of a teacher's implementation. Most of these examples portray instruction within a small group, primarily because "real" and productive conversations and discussions typically occur in the context of small- rather than large-group settings. In most instances, the excerpt is drawn from a typical classroom setting in which teachers first introduce background information and core ideas in a whole-class setting, and later "pick up" and extend instruction with a small group of students. As in most classrooms, as the teacher is working with the small group, remaining students are working independently or collaboratively on similar tasks. Finally, we conclude each example with ways for you to build on these ideas in your own classroom.

Contents

·········· **PART THREE** ··········

Writing Instruction: *Talking the Talk!*   99

PART ONE

Vocabulary Instruction
Talking the Talk!

Vocabulary knowledge is an important component of skillful reading because it influences both comprehension and fluency. That is, vocabulary knowledge allows students to quickly and accurately make sense of the text and to do so at a steady pace—without pausing or slowing down to derive the meaning of key vocabulary. The importance of vocabulary knowledge to skillful reading is reflected in the Common Core State Standards (CCSS), which include an expectation that students will be able to "interpret words and phrases" (CCSS for English Language Arts & Literacy in History/Social Studies, Science, and Technical Subjects, p. 10) in text with attention to precise meanings, and further, that students will be able to "analyze how specific word choices shape meaning or tone" (p. 10).

Vocabulary learning is most likely to occur when students are afforded multiple encounters with words in varied contexts and learning opportunities that engage them in an exploration of the multidimensional nature of words—the small and large variations in meanings that occur when words are used in different contexts and for different purposes. These encounters can be realized through firsthand experiences with topics, through conversations, and through the reading that students engage in on a daily basis.

When teaching vocabulary, the skillful teacher provides students with numerous opportunities to manipulate and learn new words through listening, speaking, reading, and writing (Beck, McKeown, & Kucan, 2002). Through these interactions with words, the teacher combines talk and instructional practices that support students' development of several aspects of word learning. He or she fosters word consciousness—the desire to learn new words and to derive satisfaction from using them—and engages students in wide reading, an avenue through which students learn many new words (Graves & Watts-Taffe, 2002). The teacher encourages connections between new and known words, and this focus, in turn, prompts students to analyze and synthesize information and to build associative conceptual understandings (Beck et al., 2002, 2008). Routine word-learning activities may include categorizing words based on prior knowledge and concept knowledge, using concept maps and webs; examining the structure of words to determine meaning (Rasinski, Padak, Newton, & Newton, 2011); or direct instruction of general and content-specific vocabulary (Beck et al., 2002). The skillful vocabulary teacher also fosters rich discussions, essential for word learning, because such discussions maximize opportunities to hear and use language while providing multiple exposures to new words (Blachowicz & Ogle, 2008; Ford-Connors, 2011). Finally, the teacher encourages students to use their understanding of word meanings to support important reading actions (e.g., inferring from context, using morphological analysis) (Graves, 2009).

In this section we provide three types of vocabulary instruction with lesson templates: (1) directly teaching word meanings; (2) inferring word meaning through context; and (3) using morphemes to understand word meaning.

Directly Teaching Word Meanings

What Is It?

Directly teaching the meanings of individual words that are important to understanding and interpreting a particular text includes three components: (1) several exposures to a few important words, (2) definitional and contextual information about the words, and (3) teacher–student dialogue that supports deep and nuanced understandings (Beck et al., 2008; Stahl & Fairbanks, 1986).

Why Is It Important?

In a meta-analysis of 52 separate studies, Stahl and Fairbanks (1986) found that when words that are important to the overall comprehension of a selection are identified and directly taught, students' comprehension of the selection improves substantially. Moreover, such instruction supports improved comprehension of other texts as well, as important vocabulary is likely to be encountered across multiple texts and content-area materials (Nagy & Scott, 2000). Direct instruction of specific words is effective when it goes beyond providing definitional information and situates the word meaning in specific and varied contexts.

When Do I Teach It?

Directly teach new words when lack of understanding of a word or words will prevent students from understanding the overall meaning of the text and, in turn, from achieving the stated knowledge goal.

What Do I Do?

Select Words to Teach.

With so many choices present in any text, how do you know which words to teach directly? Making good choices requires consideration of the "big ideas" or knowledge goals to be drawn from the text, students' familiarity with the content, and students' general word knowledge. Graves, Juel, Graves, and Dewitz (2011) suggest four considerations to guide word choice:

1 *Is the word essential to understand the big ideas presented in the text? Will the word lend itself to the knowledge goal?* If the answer is yes, then the word is probably a good choice for instruction.

2 *Can the word's meaning be sufficiently determined through the context or structural analysis?* If the context or word parts provide sufficient clues to determine meaning, then students should practice using these clues to consolidate their independent word-learning strategies.

3 *Does the word lend itself to promoting students' contextual, morphological analysis, or dictionary skills?* When students can work with words that further these skills, our instruction facilitates their acquisition of independent word-learning strategies, and thus lessens the number of words we need to teach. For example, you might decide to teach the word *submerge* because students need to learn the prefix *sub-*.

4 *Will learning the word support reading and writing outside of the current text selection?* The more likely the word is to appear multiple times within the same text as well as in other materials (e.g., other content areas and texts), the more important it is for students to understand. Multiple exposures to a word in reading and writing increase the likelihood that students will consolidate their understanding of the word and its nuances of meaning and retain the word once it is taught (Beck et al., 2002; Fisher, Frey, & Lapp, 2009).

Set a Knowledge Goal.

Begin the lesson by establishing what students will learn about their world. Relate the selected words to the knowledge goal for the focal text.

Use Talk to Explain, Model, and Guide.

- Provide multiple exposures.
- Provide definitional and contextual information.
- Provide opportunities for dialogic talk.

Recap and Reflect.

Remind students that understanding the selected words will help them understand the overall meaning of the text.

Example: Putting the Plan into Practice

Ms. Needham is working with three fourth-grade students Adam, Greg, and Sarah, who are reading *Holes*, by Louis Sachar. First, Ms. Needham works with the students to create a Vocab-o-Gram (Blachowicz & Fisher, 2002) chart to record the key words of the story (see Figure 1.1). The following excerpt begins with the segment of the lesson that focuses on the meaning of the key word *authority*. Notice how Ms. Needham first explains the meaning of the word and then engages the three

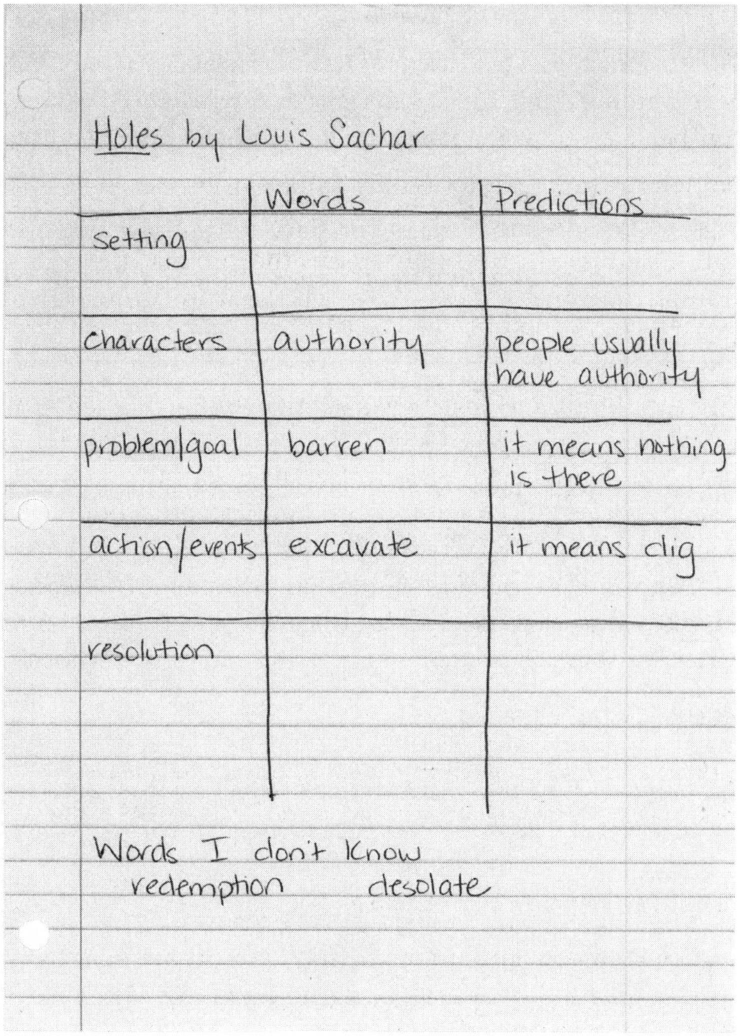

Holes by Louis Sachar

	Words	Predictions
setting		
characters	authority	people usually have authority
problem/goal	barren	it means nothing is there
action/events	excavate	it means dig
resolution		

Words I don't Know
redemption   desolate

FIGURE 1.1. Vocab-o-Gram for *Holes*, by Louis Sachar.

students in demonstrating their understanding of the word. Finally, notice how Ms. Needham engages the students in discussion of the word *authority* in relation to the characters in the text, and ends with a concluding statement about why thinking about authority is important to understanding the big ideas in this story episode.

Ms. N.: Remember our earlier discussion about the word *authority*? I'll give you a little reminder. When someone has authority, it means they have the power or right to give orders or make decisions. (*Reads word and definition on the chart paper.*) Police officers have the authority to give orders and make sure people are following the law. Your parents have the authority to make decisions about what is best for you to make sure you are safe and healthy. Who else might have authority over someone else?

GREG: Barack Obama.

Ms. N.: OK. The president. How does the president have authority?

SARAH: He can, like, make laws and things.

Ms. N.: You're right. The president has the authority to suggest laws, and then other people in our government share the responsibility in making them. Has there ever been a time when you have had authority over someone else?

GREG: I tell my sister not to use my stuff all the time.

Ms. N.: OK, but does that mean you have the authority to do that?

GREG: Yeah, if she's touching my things and I didn't say she could.

Ms. N.: Oh, so you have the authority to decide who can use things that belong to you. Do you agree, Adam? Does Greg have authority over his sister?

ADAM: Yeah, kind of. If it's his things, then he gets to decide who can use them.

Ms. N.: So Greg has the authority to say who is allowed to use things that belong to him. Let's think about *Holes* now. What does *authority* mean again?

ADAM: (*reading*) "The power or right to give orders and make decisions." So . . . so, we need the power, the power to make decisions.

Ms. N.: OK, yep, we talked about having a lot of power to make decisions, right? There are some characters in the book that have authority over others.

GREG: Oh, yeah. The campers. X-Ray is, like, the highest, like the highest . . . sort of like the leader of the campers.

Ms. N.: Great. So would you say that he has a lot of authority, or not very much authority?

GREG: A lot.

Ms. N.: Right, and being in that leadership position, he does have a lot of authority. So, I'm going to put him at the top here of this inverted pyramid [Figure 1.2]. (*Writes "X-Ray" at the top of the inverted pyramid.*) We will have a lot of characters in the middle, won't we?

SARAH: Yeah.

MS. N.: Where should Stanley fall in the amount of authority that he would have compared to other campers?

ADAM: Not a lot.

MS. N.: Not a lot, right, because—why wouldn't he have a lot?

SARAH: He was, like . . . it was just like . . . he didn't . . . he wasn't at Camp Green Lake for a really long time.

MS. N.: He was kind of like the new kid. He may not have as much power yet. He may not have, or feel that he has, a lot of power because he's so new and he can't speak up about things. OK, so we'll put Stanley toward the bottom.

The middle part is a little confusing 'cause there's so many nicknames, so many characters, but we know that the most important, the most authority would be X-Ray, and the least would be . . . ?

ALL: Stanley.

MS. N.: And we talked about people who . . . so here's campers, right? What about other people at Camp Green Lake? Which other characters have a lot of authority in this book?

SARAH: The warden. Like Mr. Pendanski said, "Don't upset the warden!"

MS. N.: Yes, so the warden. OK. Help me. Come on up here for a minute and help me to group this. We want to think about authority in relationship to another, because usually with authority . . . we're talking about power. It's power over someone or something, right? So there's always kind of someone, someone at a higher level and someone who is at a lower level here. What should we write here? We'll do this pyramid thing here. OK? So you said the warden. Where would the warden go? At the top means the most power, the most authority.

SARAH: Well, we have to move X-Ray and the campers because they don't really have the most authority. (*Crosses out and rewrites "X-Ray" and "Campers" at the bottom of the pyramid. Writes "Warden" at the top of the pyramid.*)

MS. N.: The warden. A couple of other characters who do have some authority here?

ADAM: Mr. Sir.

MS. N.: Mr. Sir? Yeah.

ADAM: (*Writes in the middle of the pyramid.*)

MS. N.: OK. Anybody else?

GREG: And then Mr. Pendanski.

MS. N.: Ah, Mr. Pendanski. Mom. Good old Mom.

GREG: (*Writes in the middle of the pyramid.*)

MS. N.: OK, so all of those, would you say that all of those characters have authority?

ADAM: Yeah.

MS. N.: Yeah. Who do they have authority over?

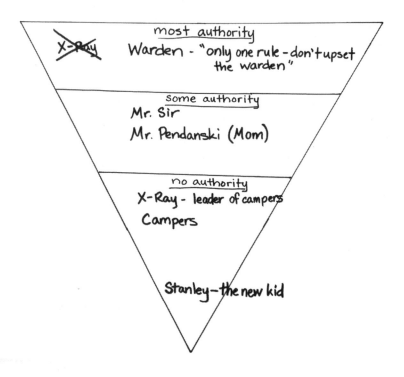

authority – the power or right to give orders or make decisions

most authority
X-Ray Warden – "only one rule – don't upset the warden"

some authority
Mr. Sir
Mr. Pendanski (Mom)

no authority
X-Ray – leader of campers
Campers

Stanley – the new kid

FIGURE 1.2. Inverted pyramid for *authority* in *Holes*.

ADAM: Campers.

MS. N.: Right, so they all have authority over the campers. Who does Mr. Sir have authority over?

SARAH: Like, Mr. Pendanski.

MS. N.: Mm-hmm, in addition to the campers. And the warden has authority over?

ADAM: Like, everybody.

MS. N.: Everybody. Everything. Great. So when we think about the authority that different characters have, it helps us to think about the relationship between the characters even more. As we continue to read, we'll need to ask ourselves if these levels of authority hold throughout the story, or if some events happen to make some characters have more or less authority. So, let's keep thinking about that as the story unfolds.

Your Turn: Talking the Talk!

1 Think about the next text your students will read. Select three to five words essential to overall understanding. Choose words that have high utility—that is, if students know the selected words, they will develop deeper understanding of the current selection; and because they will encounter the words in other texts and learning contexts, learning them now will also contribute to students' learning across the curriculum.

2 Use the lesson template (Appendix A) to help you think about and outline the language choices you will make to help students acquire deep understanding of the selected words. How will you connect learning the words to the students' knowledge goals? What student-friendly definitions will you provide for each of the words? How will you model using the words in a variety of contexts? How will you engage students in guided practice to support understanding of the words?

As you teach the lesson, audiotape it. Later, as you listen to the audiotape, reflect on each of the categories of talk: goal setting, explanatory, and feedback (Appendix B). Did you use your talk to help students set goals, to explain and prompt students to explain and share their knowledge, and to help them summarize and reflect on their learning? (See Appendix C for an example of Ms. Needham's reflections on her lesson.)

Lesson Plan 1: Directly Teaching Word Meanings

Common Core State Standard

◆ Literature Standard 4: Determine the meaning of words and phrases as they are used in a text, including those that allude to significant characters found in mythology (e.g., *Herculean*).

Text

◆ *Holes*, by Louis Sachar (Newbery Award; National Book Award)

Set the Knowledge Goal(s)

   1 How does understanding *authority* help us to understand the relationships between the characters in this story?

   2 How does understanding authority help us to understand the relationships between and among individuals in our lives?

Select Important Vocabulary

- *barren* (setting)
- *desolate* (setting)
- *excavate* (character's actions)
- *authority* (character relationships)
- *redemption* (concept; character's goal)

Justify Vocabulary Choices

- Each provides important information about essential story parts. Deep understanding of the words will help students understand the relationships between and among the essential story parts (setting, characters, goals, outcomes)

Introduce the Words

- Use a Vocab-o-Gram (Blachowicz & Fisher, 2002) (see Form 1.1 at the end of this chapter) to engage students in an initial exploration of the key words. Create a chart of the important parts of a story on the whiteboard or chalkboard and have each student create one in a notebook. Record the selected vocabulary on the chalkboard and, working in pairs, ask students to share what they know about each word and predict how the author might use the word in the selection. Will it describe the setting, a problem or a goal, a character or a character's actions, the solution to the problem or the achievement of the goal, or a consequence? After students discuss and classify words, select a few pairs to share their thinking. Use their ideas to determine students' understanding of the key words, and explain or clarify as necessary.

Explain

1 Explain that the meaning of the word *authority* is especially important in this selection. Provide or help students derive a student-friendly definition; for exmple, a person who has authority has the power or right to give orders or make decisions.

2 Provide examples of people who have authority: police officers, teachers, parents.

Guide Practice

1 Prompt students to show their understanding of the word through real-world contexts. Use statements such as the following:

- Prompting statements: "Who else might have authority over others? Has there been a time when you had authority over someone?"
- Elaborative statements: "Can you say more about that—can you give me some examples of how you exercised authority?"

- Clarifying statements: "I think I understand what you're saying, but I'm still a bit confused. Help me understand what actions or events make you think that one person has more authority than another person."

- Feedback statements: "That's a great example of someone with authority because you can really see how one person has the power or authority to make the final decision."

2 Prompt students to think about authority in relation to the characters in *Holes*. Use an inverted pyramid diagram (see Form 1.2 at the end of this chapter) to show the relationship between characters' authority and their decisions and actions. Characters with the highest amount of authority are recorded at the top of the triangle, and characters with the least are at the base of the triangle.

3 Guide practice using prompting, elaborative, clarifying, and feedback statements such as those previously described.

Recap and Reflect

- Remind students that understanding the word *authority* will help them understand the relationships between the different characters in the text and will also help THEM understand relationships between and among individuals in their lives.

Vocab-o-Gram

Name _____

Title _____ Author _____

Words

Story Element	Words	Predictions
Setting		
Characters		
Problem/Goal		
Action/Events		
Resolution		

Words I don't know

Inverted Triangle

Name _____

Definition:

When someone has **authority**, they _____

Most Authority

Some Authority

No Authority

Inferring Word Meaning through Context

What Is It?

When skilled readers encounter a word they do not know, they often use the context around the unknown word to determine at least an approximate meaning (Nagy, Anderson, & Herman, 1987). Facilitative clues to meaning can be found within the same sentence as the unknown word, within the same paragraph, in a synonym or antonym in the sentence or paragraph, or by reading on to see if the word is clarified later. Using context is a metacognitive act, as students must first recognize when meaning is compromised and then initiate a strategy to use the context to determine the word's meaning and repair comprehension (Blachowicz & Ogle, 2008).

Why Is It Important?

As students progress through school, required texts are typically more information-based and laden with unfamiliar vocabulary. When students learn to use the clues provided in the text to infer meaning, context becomes an efficient way to support comprehension and also to increase vocabulary knowledge (Fukkink & deGlopper, 1998). Studies indicate that context clue instruction is especially beneficial when combined with other word-learning strategies (e.g., morphological analysis) (Baumann et al., 2002). In addition, when paired with wide reading, students encounter more new words and, in turn, have increased opportunities to apply the word-learning strategy. Such practice, then, has a dual benefit: It contributes to vocabulary growth, and it also increases the likelihood that inferring words from context will become one of the tools in students' repertoire of reading strategies.

When Do I Teach It?

When reading or listening to text, students are unable to determine a word's meaning even when sufficient clues to meaning are provided in the text.

What Do I Do?

Select Words to Learn through Context Clues.

Words suitable to learning through context clues must be situated within text that provides clues to their meaning. These clues may be within the same sentence as the unknown word or within the same or a later paragraph. Certain types of words—those with concrete rather than abstract meanings—may be more easily understood through context clues (Schwanenflugel, Stahl, & McFalls, 1997). Moreover, since word learning typically emerges from multiple encounters with the word, context clues are unlikely to lead to deep understanding of words that appear in the text only once or twice, especially when the reader is emerging or struggling (Swanborn & deGlopper, 1999). This means that although readers might successfully use context clues to support comprehension as they read, they may not commit the word and its meaning to memory, and their "store" of vocabulary knowledge may not grow. Effective teachers, then, encourage students to use context clues as a strategy for clarifying meaning of unknown words as they read, but when focal words are such that committing them to long-term memory is important for students' ongoing learning, the teacher must also call upon other vocabulary learning strategies (e.g., direct instruction of words, morphological analysis) to support acquisition of deep vocabulary knowledge.

Set a Knowledge Goal.

Begin the lesson by establishing what students will learn about their world and explain how the use of context clues will support understanding and help them acquire world knowledge.

Use Talk to Explain, Model, and Guide.

- Describe what context clues are.
- Explain why locating and using context clues help clarify meaning.
- Model how to locate and use context clues.
- Describe the steps students can use to locate and use context clues on their own.
- Notice and name (Johnston, 2004) what students did well to figure out the meaning of an unknown word, or alternatively, what they might do the next time they encounter a new word.

Recap and Reflect.

Discuss how using context clues helped students figure out the meaning of the unknown word and connect the meaning of the word to the overall knowledge goal.

Example: Putting the Plan into Practice

In this lesson Ms. Wells is working with Ana, a third-grade student who is reading below grade level and struggles, in particular, with comprehension. Together, they are reading *The Miraculous Journey of Edward Tulane*, by Kate DiCamillo. As we enter this conversation, Ms. Wells is reading aloud, and she stops to discuss the meaning of a word that she thinks might be unfamiliar to Ana. Notice how Ms. Wells returns to the text numerous times to look for clues about the meaning of the words Ana identifies as unknown. When Ana determines the meaning, Ms. Wells again returns to the text and asks her to point out the words that helped her figure it out. Then Ms. Wells goes beyond the text, explaining a special meaning that the word carries that Ana was unlikely to be able to derive from this single example. Finally, notice how Ms. Wells places the word back into the context of the story by emphasizing how really knowing the full meaning of this word gives the reader another clue into the main character's personality.

MS. W.: (*reading aloud from the text*) "Edward, as usual, was disregarding the conversation. A breeze was blowing in off the sea and the silk scarf wrapped around his neck billowed out behind him. On his head, he wore a straw boater. The rabbit was thinking that he must look quite dashing." I see a word in that paragraph that I would like to clarify.

ANA: *Dashing.*

MS. W.: *Dashing.* We thought of the same word! So, what do you think? What can be our strategy to try and figure out what that word might mean? Hmmmm, let's reread the paragraph. Read with me.

BOTH: (*chorally reading*)

MS. W.: Right, hmmm, OK. So now let's go back to this word—*dashing*, OK?

BOTH: (*chorally reading*) "A breeze was blowing in off the sea and the silk scarf wrapped around his neck billowed off"—

ANA: Oh, I see another word, *billowed.*

MS. W.: Oh, right. What do you think that word *billowed* means?

ANA: Hmmmm.

MS. W.: So the breeze was billowing in off the sea and the silk scarf that was around his necked billowed out behind him. (*Waves hand behind her to depict something billowing in the air.*)

ANA: Oh, that means like *blowed* [sic] behind him?

Ms. W.: Exactly. Exactly, how were you able to clarify that? What were the clues in the sentence that helped you do that?

ANA: Because *billowed*, it made me think of *blow* because it has a *b* in it.

Ms. W.: OK, was there a clue in the sentence that helped you too?

ANA: Hmmmm. Well, you kinda gave me a clue because you said in the back of them and so I thought, oh, if the back of them, then that means it's blowing in the back of them.

Ms. W.: . . . and that's what it said in the sentence. It said, "It billowed out behind him." So you can get that idea that it's blowing behind him, right? OK, listen to the next sentence, or the next two sentences, and we'll talk about that word "dashing." (*reading*) "On his head, he wore a straw boater." Remember that a boater is a hat. (*Continues reading.*) "The rabbit was thinking that he must look quite dashing." Now, what do you suppose *dashing* means?

ANA: *Nice?*

Ms. W.: OK, nice. What makes you think that?

ANA: Because *dashing*, to me, I think it's a word that means *nice*. And . . .

Ms. W.: So, what made you think that? What did you have as evidence in this paragraph that might mean the word *dashing* means you look *nice*?

ANA: Because Edward likes himself a lot and he has very nice clothes, and then that would mean that he probably has nice clothes on right now, and he probably looks good, and so *dashing* would mean *looks good* or *looks nice*.

Ms. W.: That's right. Now, one more thing . . . usually, when we use the word *dashing*, it means the person looks sort of extra-nice or extra-special . . . so you get this picture in your mind of someone who's really dressed kind of special . . . would that fit what you've learned about Edward so far and the picture you have of him in your mind?

ANA: Yup. That's exactly what he looks like to me—*dashing!* Like he looks so much better than the other people around him.

Ms. W.: Great . . . I like the way you repeated the word! Let's record it up here in our character trait map of words that describe Edward.

ANA: (*Writes the word on the character trait map and continues reading with Ms. Wells.*)

Your Turn: Talking the Talk!

1 Select a group of students that needs help using context clues to derive word meaning.

2 Select a text from your current reading or content-area curriculum.

3 Begin by establishing the knowledge goal of this text. After students read, what do you expect them to know about this text and also about their world?

4 Next, read the text and identify two or three words that students are unlikely to know and that are essential to the knowledge goal. That is, if students don't understand the meanings of these words, they will not understand the big ideas of this selection. Read around the words. Will the context help students figure out the meaning of the unknown words? If so, these are good words to use to teach the strategy of using context clues.

5 Use the lesson template (Appendix A) to plan your lesson, thinking about what you will say to explain and model the strategy and also to guide students' practice of it.

6 After teaching the lesson, reflect on the explicitness and clarity of your teacher talk (Appendix B). (See Appendix C for an example of Ms. Wells's reflections on her lesson.)

Lesson Plan 2: Inferring Word Meaning through Context

Common Core State Standard

- Literature Standard 4: Determine the meaning of words and phrases as they are used in a text.
- Foundational Skills Standard 4c: Use context to confirm or self-correct word recognition and understanding, rereading as necessary.

Text

- *The Miraculous Journey of Edward Tulane*, by Kate DiCamillo (Horn Book Award)

Set the Knowledge Goal(s)

1 How does the author's word choice contribute to our understanding of the kind of person Edward is?

2 What does Edward's appearance tell us about him?

3 In the real world, do you think it's right to use the way a person looks or dresses to form opinions about that person?

Select Important Vocabulary

- *dashing*
- *billowed*

Justify Vocabulary Choices

◆ Each word contributes to a rich portrayal of the main character, Edward, whose character at the beginning of this tale is defined, at least partially, by external features—for example, his extensive wardrobe—but later, by his interactions with others and their effects on his inner being—his heart. Each word is embedded in a context that allows the reader to infer the meaning.

Explain

1 Explain that sometimes, as we read, one word holds an important clue to a "big idea" in the text. If the important word is unfamiliar, it can keep us from understanding or gaining the knowledge or information we need to make sense of the text and to understand more about our world. Often, if we pay close attention to the words and ideas around the unknown word—the context around the word—we can figure out what it means. We call this the strategy of *using context clues*.

2 Select a section of the text that includes the important words in a helpful context. Ask the students to read the section of text silently.

3 After students have read the text, direct their attention to the selected word: *dashing*. Explain that they will use context clues to determine the meaning of the word.

4 Model how to use the clues in the text to figure out the meaning of dashing.

Guide Practice

◆ Ask students to work with you to identify clues in the text that help to determine the meaning of *billows* and demonstrate how to use the clues to figure the meaning of the word.

Recap and Reflect

1 Remind students that they used context clues to determine the meaning of two important words in the text.

2 Return to the knowledge goal for the text and engage students in discussion: What does Edward's appearance tell us about him? Ask students to share their opinions and to explain how events in this selection influenced their thinking. Connect the experience to their world outside the text: In the real world, is it right to draw conclusions about a person based on appearance?

Using Morphemes
to Understand Word Meanings

What Is It?

Multisyllabic words are made of meaning-bearing parts, or morphemes (i.e., the smallest meaning-bearing units in words). Morphemes are prefixes, suffixes, roots, inflectional endings, and the smaller words within compound words. Skilled readers examine the structure of words—the morphemes—to determine the meaning of unknown words.

Why Is It Important?

Morphemic analysis, or analyzing the smaller parts in words, facilitates comprehension of word meaning, pronunciation, syntactical knowledge, spelling, and reading comprehension (Nagy, Berninger, & Abbot, 2006; Rasinski et al., 2011). Knowledge of the meanings of individual morphemes becomes a valuable word-learning resource, as students are able to apply this knowledge as they encounter unknown words as they read, and by doing so, improve their understanding of the text. As students progress through school and texts become more complex, morphological knowledge becomes increasingly important. Nagy and Anderson (1984) reported that nearly 60% of words that commonly occur in academic texts can be understood through morphological analysis. However, realizing the full benefit of morphemic knowledge requires that students join their knowledge of the meaning of common word parts with their understanding of how to use context clues. When these two skills are joined together, "for every word a child learns, . . . there are an average of one to three additional related words that should be understandable" (Nagy & Anderson, p. 304).

When Do I Teach It?

Teach strategies for analyzing words morphologically when students demonstrate little or incomplete knowledge of morphemes (i.e., prefix, suffix, root) or lack the ability to apply morphemic knowledge to derive meanings of unknown words.

What Do I Do?

Select Words to Learn through Morphological Analysis.

Words appropriate for learning through morphological analysis have a root, prefix, or suffix that students are likely to encounter repeatedly in both the selected text and in other content-area and self-selected texts.

Set a Knowledge Goal.

Begin the lesson by explaining that students will learn how analyzing and knowing about word parts contributes to our comprehension of this text and others that they will read.

Use Talk to Explain, Model, and Guide.

- ◆ Define a morpheme.
- ◆ Explain and show how to analyze words to find and use morphemes to understand new words.
- ◆ Guide students to apply morphemic analysis to unknown words.
- ◆ Notice and name (Johnston, 2004) the strategies students used to correctly solve the word meaning, or, if their efforts are unsuccessful, describe what they might do to improve their use of common word parts to derive word meanings.

Recap and Reflect.

Discuss how using the selected morpheme(s) helps readers to figure out the meaning of unknown words.

Example: Putting the Plan into Practice

In the following lesson excerpt, Ms. Matthews is working with a fifth-grade student, Bea, one on one. Bea is a fluent reader and writer with a well-developed oral vocabulary. Still, Ms. Matthews noticed that she does not always transfer her vocabulary knowledge to unknown words; more specifically, Ms. Matthews noticed that Bea does not analyze known parts in unknown words and then use that knowledge to determine the possible meanings of unknown words. As a result, Ms. Matthews decided to incorporate systematic study of Greek and Latin roots into her instructional plans for Bea. As you read the transcript, notice how Ms. Matthews begins the lesson by having Bea quickly self-assess her knowledge of the words in general. Then, even though Bea has a good grasp of the meanings of many words individually, notice how Ms. Matthews prompts her to consider the meanings of the word parts–some that she has already learned–and further facilitates her understanding through prompting her to contextualize her understanding of the words. Since this strategy had been previously introduced and modeled as part of the whole-class lesson, Ms. Matthews focuses here on guided practice.

Ms. M.: You remember that we study common roots, or morphemes, because they carry meaning, and when we know what the parts of words mean, it can help us to understand words that are unfamiliar to us. In today's lesson we're going to revisit some morphemes that we talked about previously. We are also going to talk about a new morpheme that I think will help you read and understand some new words. I wrote the word *perspective* up here on the whiteboard. In the chapter we are about to read, Vincent is going to ask Ingrid to come to the balcony to get a new "perspective." We're going to talk about the different parts or morphemes in the word *perspective* and how those parts help us figure out what the word means. But first, will you sort these words for me into familiar and unfamiliar words? (*Provides a set of word cards.*)

Bea: (*Sorts the cards.* [See Figure 3.1.])

Ms. M.: So, I noticed that you sorted the words into three piles. I wondered why.

Bea: Well, I kind of know this one. (*Points to one pile of words.*)

Ms. M.: OK. Tell me about the words you know.

Bea: So, *inspector* is a person that's, like, inspecting and looking around and making sure that whatever it is meets the standards.

Ms. M.: OK. What kind of inspectors are there?

Bea: There is maybe like house inspectors.

Ms. M.: Excellent. That's one kind of inspector. What about the next one?

Bea: A *spectator* would be like looking on.

Ms. M.: Say more . . . such as?

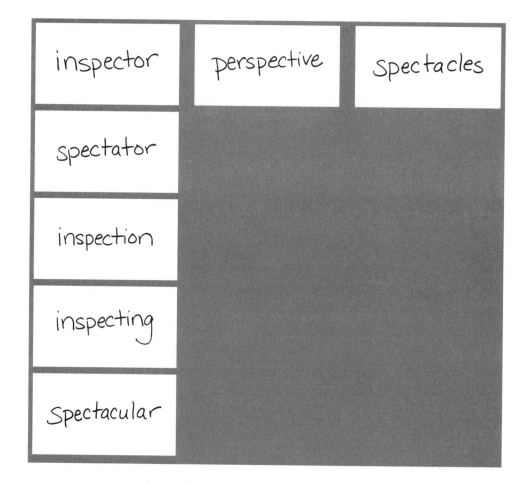

FIGURE 3.1. Word sort to assess understanding.

BEA: Like not being a part of it. Like if you're watching a game and you're on the sidelines, you're a *spectator.*

MS. M.: OK, so you're watching but not actually participating in the game.

BEA: Yeah. And then, *inspection* is the act of inspecting.

MS. M.: So how did you know it was the act of?

BEA: I think it had something to do with *-tion.*

MS. M.: You are absolutely right—you recalled that we learned in a previous lesson that *-tion* means "in the act of." So, let's look at all of the words that you sorted into your "kind of know" set. Can you tell me what all of the words have in common?

BEA: Well, they all have *spect* in them. I think it has something to do with looking.

MS. M.: So you think that *spect* might mean to look?

BEA: Yeah.

MS. M.: You're absolutely right. So here [on the whiteboard] I wrote the word *perspective.* Let's underline *spect.*

BEA: (*Underlines word part on whiteboard.*)

MS. M.: And that means?

BEA: *To look.*

MS. M.: Right, it means *to look.* Can you write *look* at the top there?

BEA: (*Writes.*)

MS. M.: OK, are there any other word parts you know?

BEA: *per?*

MS. M.: Right. We learned that *per-* is a common prefix. Will you underline it?

BEA: (*Underlines.*)

MS. M.: Do you remember what *per-* means?

BEA: Like, *through?*

MS. M.: That's right . . . will you write that above the morpheme *per?*

BEA: (*Writes.*)

MS. M.: Are there any other word parts or morphemes that you recognize?

BEA: Well, I know I've seen *ive* in some other words, but I don't really know what it means.

MS. M.: Yeah, *ive* is also a common word part—we see it in words like *attractive, explosive, captive.* But we haven't studied it and don't really know what it means yet. So, maybe we can just go ahead and see if we can figure out the meaning of *perspective* with what we already know. Based on what you know so far, what do you think *perspective* might mean?

BEA: Maybe looking through? Or seeing through?

MS. M.: OK, so when Vincent asks Ingrid to come to the balcony for a "fresh perspective" what do you suppose he means?

BEA: Well, perspective has something to do with looking through or seeing through. Vincent said "fresh," and I know that fresh can mean, like, new . . . so a fresh perspective might mean to look through or look at in a new way?

MS. M.: Exactly! You used what you know about common morphemes, and you also used other words in the sentence, to help you get at the meaning of *perspective.* When you read this part of the chapter, you'll know that Vincent is asking Ingrid to look at something in a new or different way. OK, and now that you know something about *spect*, there also will be many other words you can figure out. Let's try a few more in your set of words. If *spect* means to look, what does that tell you about the meaning of the word *spectacles?*

BEA: It has something to do with looking?

MS. M.: Yeah. Now we can add that to other context clues to determine the meaning. If a person "put on his spectacles before he started to read," what do you suppose he did??

BEA: Maybe, like, put on *glasses* or something?

MS. M.: Why do you think *glasses*?

BEA: You use them to read sometimes to help you see better.

MS. M.: Excellent. So you used your knowledge of the root *spect* and the context clues in a sentence to determine the meaning of that word. Let's try one more.

[The lesson continues with another word.]

Your Turn: Talking the Talk!

1 Select a group of students that needs help using morphological analysis to determine word meanings.

2 Use the lesson template (Appendix A) to plan your lesson, thinking about the language choices you should make to help students understand and use morphemes to determine meanings of unknown words.

- ◆ From a text you are reading, select a word that (1) is essential to overall text meaning and (2) has a common morpheme that students will encounter in other texts (e.g., *destruction*; *de*—to remove or take away; *struct*—to build; *ion*—the act of).

- ◆ Generate a list of other words that students could define if they applied morphemic knowledge (e.g., *instruction, construction, constructing, destructing*). The blank sort template in Form 3.1 at the end of this chapter can be used for this purpose.

- ◆ Talk the talk! Plan how you will model using morphemic knowledge. Pay special attention to what you will say to describe how you are analyzing word parts. As you explain, use the "language of instruction" (i.e., *morpheme, prefix, root, suffix*) to notice and name word parts and to notice and name how students are analyzing words.

- ◆ Plan how you will guide students in practice. Select or create sentences or passages in which the selected words are used meaningfully. As you guide students, emphasize *how* to look for common morphemes and how to use their understanding of the common meanings to figure out the meaning of unknown words.

- ◆ After teaching the lesson, reflect on the explicitness and clarity of your talk (Appendix B). How did it go? Did you notice and name the morphemes and the common meanings? Did you notice and name students' use of known morphemes? Appendix C provides three examples of teachers' responses to the reflection questions.

Lesson Plan 3: Using Morphemes to Understand Word Meanings

Common Core State Standard

- ◆ Literature Standard 4: Determine the meaning of words and phrases as they are used in a text, including figurative language such as metaphors and similes.
- ◆ Language Standard 4b: Use common, grade-appropriate Greek and Latin affixes and roots as clues to the meaning of a word (e.g., *photograph, photosynthesis*).

Text

- ◆ *Down the Rabbit Hole*, by Peter Abrahams

Set the Knowledge Goal

- ◆ How does analyzing the parts of words contribute to comprehension?

Select Important Vocabulary

- ◆ *perspective* (from the selection)
- ◆ *inspector*
- ◆ *inspecting*
- ◆ *inspection*
- ◆ *spectator*
- ◆ *spectacles*
- ◆ *spectacular*

Justify Vocabulary Choices

- • *Perspective* is an important concept in the chapter students are about to read and is also a term that is commonly used, especially in the study of history and other social sciences. The morpheme *spect* is common to many words in both literature and disciplinary texts, and especially common in the genre of mystery.

Explain

1 Explain that a root or a morpheme is a part of a word that carries meaning. Because some roots or morphemes are common to many different words, knowing the meanings of frequently used roots or morphemes often can help us figure out meanings of unknown words.

2 Explain that in this lesson students will learn about the morpheme *spect*.

Guide Practice

1 Prompt students to sort word cards into two categories: words that are familiar and those that are unfamiliar.

2 Prompt students to talk about what they think they know about the meanings of the words. Facilitate practice with statements such as the following:

- Elaborative statements: "Can you give me an example of what you mean?"

- Clarifying statements: "How do you know?"

3 Prompt students to examine the sorted words and consider what they all have in common. Focus attention visually to notice the common word part. Then prompt consideration of the meaning of the root *spect*, based on the meanings of the words that were sorted.

4 Focus students' attention on the word *perspective* written on the whiteboard. Ask a student to underline the word parts and then discuss the meaning of each part: *per-spect-ive*. Then combine the parts to understand the literal meaning of the word. Provide a contextual sentence for the student to either confirm meaning or to provide additional support to derive meaning.

- Prompting statements: "What does the root *spect* tell us about the meaning? What does the prefix *per-* tell us about the meaning? If we know these word parts, what might the word mean?"

- Elaborative statements: "Can you provide an example for that word?"

5 Prompt students to use what they know about the parts in the known word *(perspective)* to determine the meaning of words that are unfamiliar. Provide a contextual sentence to help derive the meanings.

Recap and Reflect

- Remind students that using known word parts can help them determine the meanings of unfamiliar words in the text. Also remind them to think about how Ingrid's "fresh perspective" might influence her actions as the mystery continues.

FORM 3.1

Blank Sort Template

Comprehension Instruction

Talking the Talk!

Comprehension, the ultimate goal of reading, is a dynamic process of nego-
tiating meaning, monitoring understanding, and connecting new ideas to
existing knowledge (Lipson & Wixson, 2009). When reading, skillful and
engaged readers do not interact only with the text itself; rather, they think
about and connect information from their own background knowledge and
join this with information in the text to build a complete and deep understanding. In addition, skillful and engaged readers often share and discuss
their developing understandings with others, as a way to further deepen their
comprehension. As explained by Baker and Wigfield (1999), "Engaged readers are motivated to read for different purposes, utilize knowledge gained
from previous experience to generate new understandings, and participate in
meaningful social interactions around reading" (p. 452). In doing so, skillful
readers read texts actively and deliberately, and they flexibly use strategies
to aid their comprehension (Duke & Pearson, 2002), often collaboratively
co-constructing deeper understandings through interactions with others
(Reznitskaya, 2012).

If we want our students to read strategically, we need to provide them
with specific strategy knowledge, explaining what the strategic actions are,
when and why the actions are likely to support meaning making, and how
to apply the strategies to varied texts (Paris et al., 1994). Then, to help students transition to independent application, we need to demonstrate how to
put this strategy knowledge to use, and to provide multiple opportunities for

scaffolded practice of the strategies with a full range of text types (Duffy, 2009; Fisher, Frey, & Lapp, 2009; Pressley, 2006). This guided strategy work facilitates students' understanding of both how and why to use particular strategies and increases the likelihood that they will gain expertise in the strategies and self-initiate their use as they read independently.

In this section we describe seven important reading comprehension strategies—(1) visualizing, (2) making inferences, (3) determining what's important, (4) making predictions, (5) making connections, (6) summarizing, and (7) close reading—and provide examples of lessons that incorporate teacher talk that helps students acquire and use the strategies.

Lesson 4

Visualizing

What Is It?

When readers visualize while reading, they create mental pictures of what they have read, responding to the descriptive language used by the author (Duffy, 2009). According to Duffy (2009), visualizing—or *imaging*, as he labels it—requires that readers access their prior knowledge of concepts, experiences, and descriptive language and predict through mental pictures what those details made you think.

Why Is It Important?

Akin to watching a movie in your mind, visualizing while reading is a valuable strategy, especially when reading narrative text (Duke & Pearson, 2002; Duffy, 2009). In particular, studies have found that students in grade 3 and beyond experience improved reading comprehension when they work at visualizing the images described in the text (Tierney & Cunningham, 1984). Moreover, students who are acquiring English as a second language report relying on mental images to help them clarify and understand as they read (Jiménez, García, & Pearson, 1995). When readers create images from words on the page, the texts come alive as readers see, hear, or feel the actions of characters in particular settings. As they immerse themselves more deeply in the text, they are likely to sustain motivation and engagement in the text and to become hooked by the power of reading (Blachowicz & Ogle, 2008; Duffy, 2009).

When Do I Teach It?

When listening to a text read aloud or reading text, students are unable to accurately describe what is happening, and they don't seem to be noticing the author's word choices that they could use to help them to form images in their minds.

What Do I Do?

Select a Text Appropriate for Visualization.

Visualization supports reading comprehension when the words on the page are such that forming a mental picture of the image is likely to deepen understanding and cause the characters, places, or events to come alive in the reader's mind. As you prepare to introduce this strategy, think about the language of various texts and select from among those—narrative or expository—that are likely to evoke rich images. Among our favorites are the books of William Steig (especially *Amos and Boris*, with the image of Boris becoming "breaded with sand" as the elephants roll him over and over and back into the sea); the informational book *Mud*, by Mary Lyn Ray, with its description of "gooey, gloppy, mucky, magnificent mud"; and the informational book *Night Shift*, by Jessie Hartland, with its rich descriptions of evening jobs: "under any inky-black sky the truck driver swiftly loads up perishable freight." (See Appendix D for a short list of books that we recommend to teach visualization.)

Set a Knowledge Goal.

Begin the lesson by establishing what the students will learn about their world. Relate visualizing to the knowledge goal.

Use Talk to Explain, Model, and Guide.

- Define visualization and explain how readers use authors' words to create mental images, and when and why it might help them to deepen their understanding and enjoyment of text.

- Using the focal text, select some excerpts that are rich in opportunities for visualization and model for students how you use the author's words to form a picture in your mind.

- Select additional excerpts to share and engage students in discussion of the images the words evoke. Prompt students to describe what they see and how the image contributes to their understanding of the others ideas.

Recap and Respond.

Remind students that visualizing or using the author's words to form mental images or "pictures in your mind" often helps us to understand the overall meaning of the text.

Example: Putting the Plan into Practice

Mr. Peterson is working with four fourth-grade students, Ariv, Kelly, Dominic, and Jack, who are reading *The Hundred Dresses*, by Eleanor Estes. In the following excerpt, notice how he first reminds the students of the goal they have for reading this book and then explains how they are going to visualize while reading to help them reach their goal. Notice too, as the lesson unfolds, how he uses his talk to skillfully frame the discussion, sometimes using his comments and questions to guide students to think about specific events or even words that the author uses, sometimes using his talk to revoice or rephrase what students say and prompt elaboration, and sometimes to provide feedback that affirms the strategies he observed them using.

MR. P.: So, *The Hundred Dresses*, and we left off on page 50, right? Remember, we've been reading this story, thinking about how our words and actions affect people either positively or negatively. Today we're going to visualize as we are reading to think more about our goal, but I think it's a good idea before we start reading new passages, to recap what it was we read in the last passage. This way we get ourselves back into the story and remember important story events before we continue reading. So, can someone tell me a little bit about what was going on in the story the last time you read?

ARIV: Peggy . . . no, not Peggy, Wanda—she didn't show up at school because it said the parents said she couldn't come back because they were making fun of her.

MR. P.: OK. They were making fun of her about what?

ARIV: About, like, she wore only one dress.

KELLY: Also because of her last name.

MR. P.: So, she wore only one dress.

ARIV: And her last name.

MR. P.: And what do you think it means? Can you make an inference about her and her family, if she had only one dress?

DOMINIC: Well, she feels really embarrassed 'cause she has to wear it all the time.

MR. P.: Wanda feeling embarrassed is a good inference, because kids at school see her wearing the same clothes all the time. It makes her stand out a little.

DOMINIC: And upset, because people keep sort of insulting her, like everyone jokes about her.

MR. P.: So, this girl Wanda has one dress, and you said, Ariv, that her family moved away because . . .

ARIV: Because she was getting teased.

MR. P.: OK. Anything else happen, Dominic, since the last time we read?

DOMINIC: Well, she said that she has a hundred dresses—

MR. P.: —Mmhm.

DOMINIC: —and that's sort of a lie.

MR. P.: It's a lie?

KELLY: But she does.

DOMINIC: But she just said that because she doesn't want people teasing her so much.

MR. P.: Good. She's trying to get people to stop teasing her.

DOMINIC: And she said that she doesn't bring 'em because she doesn't want them to get dirty. She only brings them at parties.

MR. P.: Dominic made another inference there, right? He said that she was lying, and that she didn't want to be teased about it. The author doesn't really say that, but you can figure it out, that's why.

JACK: She wasn't exactly lying—

MR. P.: What do you mean?

JACK: —because she had a hundred dresses that she *drew*.

MR. P.: OK. So she drew pictures of a hundred dresses.

JACK: And every single dress that she mentioned was on the—

MR. P.: On the pictures?

JACK: Yeah.

MR. P.: That's a good point, too. So, right, at the end of page 50, the two girls,—

JACK: They went up to Baggins Hill to see . . .

MR. P.: Maddie and Peggy, what were they going to do? What were they gonna do?

KELLY: They were going to Boggins Heights to see if they were still there.

MR. P.: OK. So what do you think? Anybody have a prediction?

DOMINIC: Well, I think Wanda might not be there—

MR. P.: She won't be there?

DOMINIC: —'cause she did, like, move away.

MR. P.: OK. So, what have Peggy and Maddie realized about their words and actions? Let's read on to find out. Before you start, though, we just talked a little bit about visualizing when we were together on the rug. Remember, you visualize when you make a picture in your head of what the author is saying. You use the author's words and what you know already to make a picture in your head. I'd like you to take a minute when you're done reading on to page 51 to read it a second time, and after reading it a second time, close your eyes and see if you can picture the author's description. What do the author's words help you to see in your head? How does picturing what's happening help you learn more about the character's feelings?

STUDENTS: (*reading silently*)

MR. P.: OK. Can you picture that at all? From that description, what do you see? Can you describe it?

ARIV: Two girls running up the hill trying to get somewhere. And it's raining.

MR. P.: And it's raining. OK. You want to add anything to that, Dominic?

DOMINIC: No, 'cause I'm not good at picturing things in my head.

MR. P.: No? Have you just ever, I know it's now January, but in the book, what time of year are they doing this in?

ARIV: November.

MR. P.: November. OK. And, can you remember back to November? What words does the author use to describe the day?

DOMINIC: Uh, let's see. Like it's *drizzly, damp,* and *dismal.*

MR. P.: *Drizzly, damp,* and *dismal.* OK. So can you sort of see the cold, wet, gray kind of day in your head?

DOMINIC: (*Nods.*)

MR. P.: All right, it's a damp, drizzly day. Let's continue reading through the next page. Keep picturing in your mind what is happening and how the characters are feeling.

STUDENTS: (*reading silently*)

MR. P.: It's damp. It's drizzly. How do you guys think Maddie is feeling? If you could describe the way she's feeling about the situation, what would you say?

KELLY: Kind of sad and ashamed.

ARIV: Guilty.

KELLY: —that she make her leave.

MR. P.: I love that, *ashamed,* and what did you guys say?

DOMINIC: *Guilty.*

MR. P.: Guilty. Why does she feel guilty?

JACK: They made fun of her.

ARIV: They made fun of her and now she's leaving.

DOMINIC: They made fun of her so many times. Yeah.

MR. P.: And does she wish she could change it?

ARIV: Yeah.

JACK: Because it says she and Peggy would fight anyone who was not nice.

MR. P.: Right. There's the evidence. I like how Jack went back into the text and pulled out those words that support his inference. That was good.

[The lesson continues with further guided practice.]

Your Turn: Talking the Talk!

1 Think about the next text your students will read for which visualizing would be a useful strategy to facilitate understanding.

2 Use the lesson template (Appendix A) to help you think about and outline the language choices you should make to incorporate the characteristics of effective teacher talk. How will you connect this strategy work to the students' purpose for reading and general knowledge goals? How will you explain and model how to visualize? How will you engage the students in guided practice of visualizing to deepen their understanding of characters or events?

3 As you teach your lesson, audiotape it. As you later listen to the audiotape, reflect on each of the categories of talk: goal setting, explanatory, and feedback (Appendix B). Did you use your talk to help students set goals, to explain and prompt students to read strategically and share their emerging understanding of the story, and to provide facilitative feedback? (See Appendix C for Mr. Peterson's reflections on his lesson.)

Lesson Plan 4: Visualizing

Common Core State Standard

♦ Literature Standard 3: Describe in depth a character, setting, or event in a story or drama, drawing on specific details in the text (e.g., a character's thoughts, words, or actions).

Text

♦ *The Hundred Dresses*, by Eleanor Estes (Newbery Award Honor Book)

Set the Knowledge Goal(s)

1 How does visualizing help us understand the characters, setting, and events in this story?

2 How do our words and actions affect other people?

Explain

1 Review important information about events in the story from the previous reading session. Explain how this reviewing helps a reader get back into a story before reading the next sections.

2 Explain that the students visualize—picture places, characters, and events in their minds—while reading the story to deepen their understanding about the characters' feelings. When readers visualize, they use the descriptive details from the text and their own background knowledge to create mental pictures of what is happening in the story.

Guide Practice

1 Prompt the students to summarize important information from the previous day's reading.

2 Prompt students to predict what will happen now as they continue to read.

3 Prompt students to visualize while reading the next page and to think about how visualizing helps them understand the characters' feelings. Guide practice with statements such as the following:

- ◆ Prompting statements: "What part of this episode helped you picture in your head how the characters are feeling? What did the author do to help you form that image? What did you do to help you form that image?"

- ◆ Elaborative statements: "Can you say more about how picturing those details help you understand how the character is feeling? OK, [Name] is saying _____. Does anybody have anything to add to that?"

- ◆ Clarifying statements: "I'm not sure I understand how picturing those details are helping you here. Let's go back to the text and check."

- ◆ Feedback statements: "So those details there really give you a picture in your mind of how Maddie is feeling about teasing Wanda. That's great."

Recap and Respond

1 Remind the students that visualizing the characters, setting, and events will help them deepen their understanding of the characters' feelings and motivations.

2 Prompt students to think about the knowledge goal and to record a response in their reading notebooks: Based on what you have read today, how do our words and actions affect other people?

Making Inferences

What Is It?

Making inferences while reading involves figuring out what the author left unsaid—reading between the lines to fully understand the author's meaning (Duffy, 2009). To make inferences, readers must look for and draw upon evidence and clues in the text and combine those specific details with their own background knowledge.

Why Is It Important?

Authors often do not tell us everything we need to know to make sense of their text; rather, they typically omit information they expect readers already know. Doing otherwise, said Hansen (1981), might cause authors to "be regarded as pedantic bores!" (p. 393). They depend, then, on readers to fill in the holes or missing information by searching for hints and clues in the text and connecting these with their own background knowledge and experiences to fully understand the author's ideas. This ability to "fill in the holes" by making inferences is a fundamental part of many strategic reading actions, such as predicting, making connections, visualizing, and drawing conclusions. Making inferences helps readers to delve deeply into the details of narrative texts to understand critical aspects of a story—for example, the relationships between and among place and time, characters and their actions, or outcomes and consequences. When the text is expository, making inferences facilitates critical thinking and evaluation, leading readers to consider, for example, the relationship between an author's background and viewpoint and the veracity of ideas and claims in a text. In short, making inferences is fundamental to the type of close reading that leads to successful and deep comprehension—the type of reading that is now demanded by the CCSS (National Governors Association Center for Best Practices and Council of Chief State School Officers, 2010).

The importance of explicitly teaching students how to make logical inferences is important, then, because so much of what we do as readers requires us to read between the lines to fully understand the author's meaning (Duffy, 2009; Pressley, 2006). Moreover, explicitly teaching students to make logical inferences is important because some readers—those who are younger and also those who are older, struggling readers—are capable of making inferences, but they are less likely to do so without prompting and scaffolding (Cain & Oakhill, 2007).

When Do I Teach It?

When listening to a narrative text read aloud or reading a narrative text, students are unable to make logical inferences based on the author's implied ideas and their own background knowledge and experiences.

What Do I Do?

Select an Appropriate Text.

Almost any text invites the reader to make inferences, but in some, the author uses a style that demands that readers infer to fully understand the text. Consider, for example, Karen Kaufman Orloff's, *I Wanna Iguana*. The main character, Alex, writes a letter to his mom, explaining why he should take his friend's baby iguana when his friend moves. In response, his mom writes a letter acknowledging Alex's concern, offering assurance that the iguana will be safely cared for by someone else, and ending with the words, "Nice try, though." Readers must read between the lines to fully understand and interpret his mom's comments. From page to page, Alex and his mom continue this conversation through letter writing, with each letter demanding that readers make inferences to fully comprehend the text. Taking meaning only from the words on the page will leave the reader with only partial understanding, and will likely diminish the reader's comprehension and enjoyment of the text. Texts such as this are an especially effective resource for introducing the strategy of making inferences, as page by page, the reader experiences the importance of "reading between the lines." (See Appendix E for other children's and young-adult literature titles that lend themselves to teaching students to infer.)

Set a Knowledge Goal.

Begin the lesson by establishing what the students will learn about their world. Relate making inferences to the knowledge goal.

Use Talk to Explain, Model, and Guide.

◆ Define *making inferences* and explain how readers use authors' words, their own background knowledge and experiences, and sometimes illustrations to construct meaning that is not explicitly stated. (See Figure 5.1 for a basic "formula" for making inferences.)

◆ Using the focal text, select an episode or excerpt that is likely to lead to incomplete or misunderstanding unless the reader "reads between the lines" and makes an inference. Model for students how you use the author's words and your own knowledge and experience (and the illustration, if appropriate) to make an inference.

◆ Select a new episode or excerpt to read together and engage students in discussion of clues and hints in the text and information outside the text that might lead them to form a particular inference. Emphasize the importance of combining both text-based and reader-based information. Continue with additional episodes or excerpts until you observe that students are effectively combining information in the text and information outside the text to make logical inferences.

Recap and Respond.

Remind students that making inferences will help them understand the meaning the author was really trying to convey.

Example: Putting the Plan into Practice

This example is drawn from a teacher's interaction with one student. Ms. Masters is working with a sixth-grade student, Eileen, in an intervention setting. She is reading *Monsoon Summer*, by Mitali Perkins, a text that coheres with Eileen's current social studies curricular content on Indian and Indian American culture and current English focus on making inferences to understand character motivations and

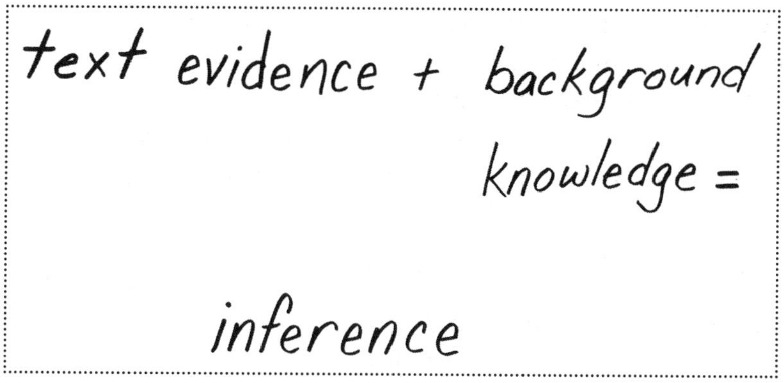

FIGURE 5.1. Formula for making inferences.

change over the course of stories. In the following excerpt, notice how Ms. Masters first queries Eileen about what she knows about making inferences, and then how she explains that making inferences is an important strategy to use when reading stories and to learn more about her goals from social studies class. Ms. Matthews and Eileen then co-construct the explanation using examples of inferring outside of the text to understand what it means to make an inference about a character.

Ms. M.: All right. You mentioned that you remember Ms. Taylor [English teacher] talking about inferences while reading. Do you remember what she may have talked about with inferences?

EILEEN: No, 'cause it was a few days ago. I just remember her mentioning that word.

Ms. M.: OK. Well, inferring is sometimes a hard strategy to use when reading, but it is also very important, especially when reading stories. So what we're going to be doing here is to practice making some inferences while we continue to read *Monsoon Summer*, because inferring will help us to understand how Jazz is dealing with fitting into life in India and how she is feeling about making those choices to fit in with the other girls in the community. An inference is what I have in this equation up on the board [text evidence + background knowledge = inference (Figure 5.1)], when you take what the text says and add in your own background knowledge and all your experiences that you've ever had before, and you use it to learn something new about the text that the author doesn't tell you. It's kind of like, if you've ever heard the expression "reading between the lines."

EILEEN: I've heard of it, but I don't know what it means.

Ms. M.: Well, authors, when they're writing books, rarely tell us every single thing.

EILEEN: Oh.

Ms. M.: They leave some things for your imagination and some things for you to figure out from other clues in the text.

EILEEN: On your own?

Ms. M.: On your own, yes. And that figuring out on your own is called *inferring*.

EILEEN: Oh! So like when they use those phrases, the ones that you said were going to be hard in the book *Code Orange*.

Ms. M.: Oh, like metaphors and things?

EILEEN: Yeah, yeah, yeah. Like they want you to figure out on your own what that's supposed to mean.

Ms. M.: Kind of. They want you to *infer* how she's feeling based on that language and what it says in the text. An example is if Sally is in the corner over there crying, what can we infer about her?

EILEEN: Somebody hurt her.

Ms. M.: OK. Maybe somebody hurt her.

EILEEN: Something hurt her.

MS. M.: OK. So somebody or something hurt her. Could be either. What might give you another clue? What could you look for to figure out whether it was somebody or something?

EILEEN: Well, maybe if it was something, she'd be rubbing, like, her arm or her leg or her head. But if she's not holding on or rubbing any part of her, then, probably, it's like—sort of like just her feelings are hurt. And so it was probably someone who hurt her.

MS. M.: Good. That's it! You look for clues that help you figure out what could be going on when you have only part of the information. Let's just say that she's not holding any part of her body, so probably someone said or did something to hurt her. How do you think she's feeling?

EILEEN: Sad. Or she could be happy crying, but probably sad.

MS. M.: Well, now, that's another interesting possibility. Sometimes we cry from happiness. Is there some hint or something that would help us know the difference between happy crying and sad crying?

EILEEN: Yeah . . . usually if someone is crying cuz of something good, there are both tears and smiles. If it's bad, it's just lots of tears.

MS. M.: All right, so let's say that with Sally, we don't see any smiles—just lots tears. We can say that Sally is sad. Now does she have to be in the corner yelling, "I'm sad! I'm sad! I'm sad!" for you to figure out that she's sad?

EILEEN: No.

MS. M.: No. So that's you making an *inference* based on her behavior and what she's doing. Inferences can be taken from what characters do—their actions, what they say, and how they say it.

EILEEN: Yes, but sometimes you can also tell in the way somebody moves because they're walking down the hall in a weird way or something.

MS. M.: Mm-hmm.

EILEEN: And that's how you can also tell by body language.

MS. M.: Right, so body language can also be considered something that they're doing, an action—you're absolutely right. You can make an inference from someone's body language.

EILEEN: Oh.

MS. M.: What if you walked in here and I was like throwing pens into the bin and tossing papers all over the place, and you came in and I was like "How are you?" (*in an aggravated tone*) like that? You could infer that my mood was . . .

EILEEN: Not so good.

MS. M.: Not so good, yes. How do you know if I don't tell you, "Oh, I'm in a bad mood!"

EILEEN: Because of what you're doing with the pens and stuff and how you sound mad.

MS. M.: Right, you could just tell. You could kind of figure it out from my actions and what I said because you have probably had experiences like that before in your life. So that's what we're going to be trying to do with *Monsoon Summer* here. We'll be making some inferences about Jazz and the other characters to help us figure out what's really happening—to fill in the gaps that the author is leaving for us. What I'm going to do now is start to read Chapter Four, and I'm going to show you how we make inferences. After I'm done, I'm going to have you read a little bit on your own and see if you can work through making an inference yourself. All right?

EILEEN: OK.

MS. M.: Chapter Four; What's happened? Give me a little background information.

EILEEN: She has just left because she's going to pack for India, and she just left the lunchroom and Marian was making Jazz feel bad because she's leaving for India. And she's doing the "Oh! I didn't know you were . . . " She's being a faker.

MS. M.: She's a big faker because what does she want?

EILEEN: She wants Steve. Jazz is having the problem, but Steve is kind of a little bit creating the problem? Because everybody likes him. But Marian's helping him.

MS. M.: All right, so let's take a look. (*Reads a brief section of the text aloud.*) So, we know the text tells us that they want to change their minds, right? But it doesn't tell us exactly why—I wonder why the grandparents don't want them to go. I know that the parents or the grandparents never go outside their gated community, because the author told us that way back in the first chapter. So the inference that I'm making is that they're nervous or scared for their family. They think something bad could happen to them in India. 'Cause it's not like they're just going outside their community, you know? Jazz and her parents are going halfway across the world. Does that make sense?

EILEEN: Yeah.

MS. M.: So, the inference is that Grandma and Grandpa are scared for Jazz and her family. Making these inferences will help us learn more about why the characters do what they do. Let's continue reading to find out more about the trip and the problems that are arising. In this next part think about how Jazz is reacting to this trip.

EILEEN: Not good either.

MS. M.: Right. She doesn't really want to go and be away from Steve. Let's continue reading to find out more about the trip and the problems with Jazz and Steve.

[The lesson continues with further guided practice on making inferences.]

Your Turn: Talking the Talk!

1 Think about the next narrative text your students will read for which making inferences would be an important strategy to support understanding.

2 Use the lesson template (Appendix A) to help you think about and outline the language choices you should make to incorporate the characteristics of effective teacher talk. How will you connect this strategy work to the students' reading goals? How will you explain and model how to infer? How will you engage the students in guided practice of inferring to clarify important ideas and relationships?

3 As you teach your lesson, audiotape it. Later, as you listen to the audiotape, reflect on each of the categories of talk: goal setting, explanatory, and feedback (Appendix B). Did you use your talk to help students set goals, to explain and prompt students to read strategically and share their emerging understanding of the story, and to provide facilitative feedback? Appendix C provides three examples of teachers' responses to the reflection questions.

Lesson Plan 5: Making Inferences

Common Core State Standard

◆ Literature Standard 1: Cite textual evidence to support analysis of what the text says explicitly as well as inferences drawn from the text.

Text

◆ *Monsoon Summer*, by Mitali Perkins

Set the Knowledge Goal(s)

1 Draw inferences that help understand how a person's cultural background and experiences shape learning and experiences in a new culture.

2 Is a willingness to take chances a positive character trait?

Explain

1 Explain that students will be making inferences while reading the story in order to understand the characters' motivations, traits, and feelings. When readers infer, they use evidence from the current and previous episodes and combine it with their own background knowledge to read between the lines and gain a deeper understanding of the story. Use Form 5.1 at the end of this chapter to guide students through the inference-making process.

2 Provide examples, derived from outside the text, of inferring feelings from people's actions and words.

3 Model how to infer the feelings of the grandparents, citing evidence from the text to show why the inference makes sense.

Guide Practice

◆ Prompt students to infer how the characters are acting and feeling based on the textual evidence at predetermined stopping points. Guide practice with statements such as the following:

◆ Prompting statements: "So, what are you thinking about Jazz now? What can you infer about what just happened?"

◆ Elaborative statements: "Why do you think so? Can you show me where the text led you to think that? How do you know?"

◆ Clarifying statements: "I don't think she is _____ here. Let's take another look at that section to see if we can find clues that help us understand why Jazz is acting that way."

◆ Feedback statements: "Good. I like how you connected Jazz's action there to what happened earlier in the story. That helped you make an inference here about how Jazz is feeling."

Recap and Respond

1 Remind students that inferring involves reading between the lines, using text evidence and background knowledge in order to learn more about characters' traits, motivations, and feelings.

2 Prompt students to reflect orally on the knowledge goal: Have we learned anything yet about how a willingness to take chances may lead to positive changes?

Making Inferences

Name _____

Title _____ Author _____

Text Evidence	+	Background Knowledge	=	Inference

Determining What's Important

What Is It?

Determining what is important involves knowing how to sift through the wealth of information provided in texts and knowing why certain facts and details are more important than others. This discernment is always important, but even more so when reading expository texts that are often lengthy and densely filled with information. When skilled readers read an informational text, they are sometimes able to use the text's structure (e.g., comparison–contrast, cause–effect, main idea–details) and features as guideposts to help them focus on the most important details and ideas to remember. At other times, readers must rely on their prior knowledge to make decisions about what is important and what is trivial.

Why Is It Important?

Understanding and using this strategy is essential because texts contain much more information than readers are able to focus on, remember, and learn (Pressley, 2006; Pressley & Afflerbach, 1995). Therefore, skilled readers need to be able to use the features and structure of a text, as well as be able to make judgments based on their prior knowledge, to determine which aspects of the text are most important. However, studies indicate that readers—even those who are seemingly capable— are often unable to determine what is important as they read. In fact, students are often more likely to recall "seductive details (i.e., highly interesting but relatively unimportant)" (Jetton & Alexander, 1997, p. 290) at the expense of the important information. Moreover, studies indicate that teachers may have substantial influence on how students differentiate important and unimportant information in text. That is, students tend to pay attention to what their teachers value as important (Alexander, Jetton, Kulikowich, & Woehler, 1994); and these values don't always cohere with the structurally important information in the text (Jetton & Alexander, 1997). When teachers fail to appropriately identify and emphasize important ideas in the text, students tend to fail in this regard as well. So the task for teachers is twofold: (1) They must teach students a strategy for distinguishing important from trivial information as they read, and (2) their instruction must consistently emphasize the structurally important information in the text. Finally, students may be more likely to distinguish important from trivial information when they are somewhat familiar with and interested in the topic. So, when assigning lengthy or conceptually dense texts, teachers should pay special attention to building requisite background knowledge about the text and to identifying reading purposes that have clear and important relevance to students' own lives.

When Do I Teach It?

Explicitly teach strategies for identifying and recalling important information in text when you observe that students recall and share information without any attention to the "weight" or importance of the ideas.

What Do I Do?

Select an Appropriate Text.

Although our goal is for readers to focus on important information in every text they read, deliberately and intentionally exercising this strategy is more important when reading texts that are likely to be somewhat challenging for students to comprehend and recall. For example, informational text that is conceptually dense or especially long (or both!) can place an overwhelming "memory load" on readers, especially if their inclination is to try to remember everything they read. This attempt often results in students' understanding and recalling very little of what they read, and such an experience with comprehension failure, in turn, often results in diminished motivation to read. When we demonstrate to students that applying this strategy to an otherwise challenging text can bring the text within their reach, we help them to recognize that using the strategy has the potential to help them achieve their knowledge goals.

Set a Knowledge Goal.

Begin the lesson by explaining how determining importance of ideas will help them sort through all of the information in text and identify the ideas that will deepen their understanding of the main topic.

Use Talk to Explain, Model, and Guide.

◆ Describe how to distinguish between important and trivial information in text.

◆ Explain and show how to use the text's structure and features to focus on important information; or alternatively, how to use their particular purpose (or the teacher's purpose) to focus on important information.

◆ Guide students as they apply their awareness of text structure and text features (or their particular purpose for reading) to distinguish important from unimportant information.

◆ Notice and name (Johnston, 2004) strategies the students use during reading and describe how their actions support comprehension and achievement of their knowledge goals.

Recap and Reflect.

Discuss how distinguishing important from trivial information helps students to achieve their learning goals.

Example: Putting the Plan into Practice

In the following lesson excerpt, Mr. Garrison is working with a small group of fourth-grade students, Aiden, Max, Nathaniel, and Karen, on determining important information when reading an informational text about the North American colony of Pennsylvania. This excerpt is from the second lesson Mr. Garrison taught to this particular group. The students first worked with this strategy when reading about the Massachusetts colony the previous day. As you read the transcript, notice how Mr. Garrison first establishes the knowledge goal questions that are framing their study of the colonies. Then, notice how he briefly explains how they will use those questions, along with the headings in the text, to determine what is most important to remember. (Figure 6.1 is a chart that illustrates this organizational strategy.) Finally, notice that when Aiden initially responds with information not entirely relevant to the key questions, Mr. Garrison redirects the students' focus, cueing them to revisit two pages that would support understanding of the key questions.

MR. G.: I've given everybody a copy of the *Pennsylvania* book, part of our National Geographic series. What I'd like you to do is open it up and scan it. Take a look at the cover. Look at the headings, the pictures, maps, those features.

ALL: (*previewing the text*)

AIDEN: This book is really informational.

MR. G.: Right. This book is nonfiction, and it's part of a series on different colonies. If you open it up, you see the inside cover. There's some information there about

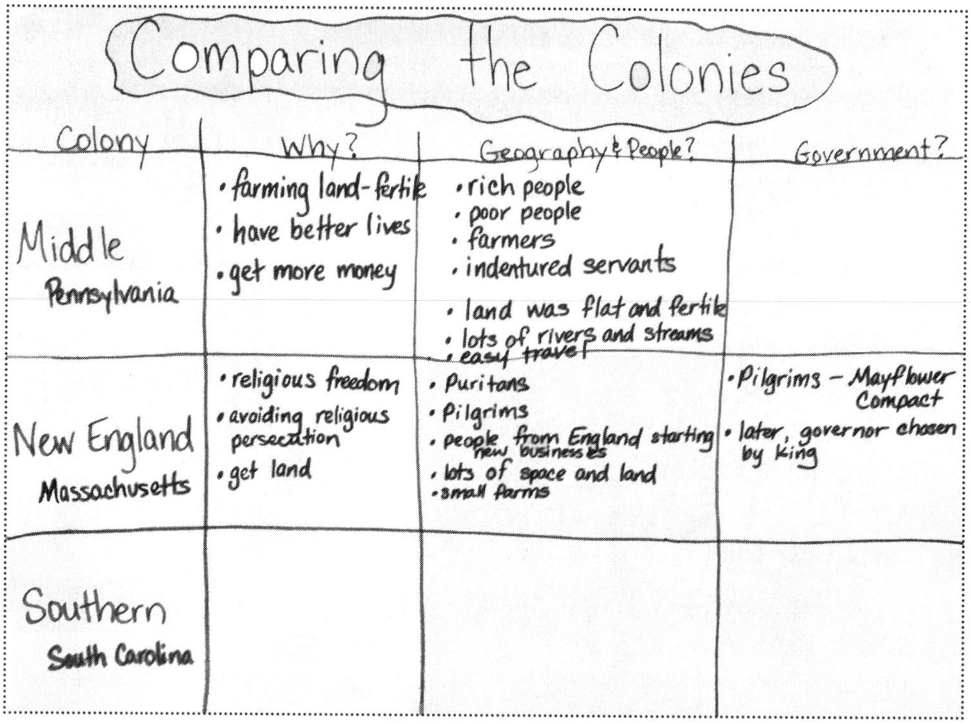

FIGURE 6.1. Ms. Garrison's colony comparison chart.

three key concepts. There are three things that they really want you to think about as you read this, OK? First, people moved to and settled in North American colonies for several reasons. Second, each colony was influenced by its geography and people. And third, in time, North American colonies grew larger and wealthier and began to govern themselves. Those three concepts are going to be the same three concepts in all of the books on the different colonies because they are the really big ideas to understand about why and how people colonized North America. We are going to read today to find information related to these three ideas for Pennsylvania because then we will be able to compare this colony to the other colonies we are learning about.

OK. So, pages 6 through 16 are all about just Pennsylvania and how it grew from a beginning colony to a more established colony—sort of the history of Pennsylvania. OK? If you turn to page 21, from page 21 to the end is all about one person, William Penn. As we read these two sections, I want you to think about the information that you are reading, and I want you to think about these three big ideas about the colonies. Finding information about these big ideas will be important information to contribute to our understanding of the colonies in North America. There will likely be other information in this text as well, but we want to focus on what's most important, just like we were doing yesterday when we met. As you read for this information, the headings and subheadings are going to help you predict what's in each of the sections. By looking at the heading, you can tell what the main idea of the paragraph might be, which can help you more easily determine what is important to remember.

OK. I want you to start reading from page 6 to page 13, thinking about these three ideas.

STUDENTS: (*Read silently.*)

MR. G.: OK. So, did we learn any important information in that section that you read so far? Remember, our three big ideas are related to why people settled, how the geography and people influenced life, and how they began to govern themselves.

AIDEN: That they're split up into different sections called *colonies*, and that there's . . . that Pennsylvania is in the middle colonies, and there's the New England colonies and the southern and middle colonies.

MR. G.: OK. So this section gave us an overview of the different colonies. Did they give a hint at all about that key concept . . . that first key concept? Was any information there about why the people may have wanted to move?

AIDEN: Not really.

MR. G.: Not yet? OK. We want to be keeping an eye out for that 'cause it's one of the things they're telling you is really important. Let's look at these two pages. What would you say the main idea is of these two pages?

MAX: It tells why people came to Pennsylvania.

MR. G.: OK. What did you learn?

AIDEN: And who they were.

MR. G.: And who they were. OK. Right. The heading clues us in to important information here.

AIDEN: (*reading*) "People Who Came to Pennsylvania."

MR. G.: And then the subheadings are all what?

AIDEN: (*reading*) "Types of People."

MR. G.: "Types of People," right? So you want to use those clues. What did you learn?

JENNIFER:: People moved for farming land and to have better lives.

MR. G.: Oh, so they came to Pennsylvania for good farming land and to be able to make better lives for themselves.

NATHANIEL: People came to try to be wealthier, and poor people came to get money.

MR. G.: (*laughing*) OK. So the rich people just wanted to get richer, and the poor people just wanted to get better than they were. What else did you learn?

NATHANIEL: That there was a really big variety of people coming to Pennsylvania.

MR. G.: OK. What do you mean by *variety*? Who was coming?

NATHANIEL: Rich people, poor people, farmers.

MR. G.: OK. I like how you were going back to the text, finding those subtitles that tell you who the different people were. Aiden, what about you? Did you learn anything that you didn't know?

AIDEN: Well, that an indentured servant is like someone who gets paid . . . like they have someone pay for their fare to go to the New World, and then they have to work for them for a few years or something. And then they get to get their own land and clothes and everything.

MR. G.: Mm-hmm. And during the time when they're working for the other person, they get their fare paid for and they agree to work for the person for a certain number of years. What else is important to note about indentured servants?

AIDEN/MAX: They don't get paid.

MR. G.: They're not getting paid at all. They're working for free basically to pay off their debt. What about our second idea of the influence of geography?

JENNIFER:: They're talking about how the land was flat and the land had lots of rivers, and it was small. And a little about history.

MR. G.: OK. So, go back to this paragraph here about Pennsylvania has lots of streams and rivers. Does this relate to one of our big ideas?

NATHANIEL: Yeah, geography.

MR. G.: Why it has streams and rivers. Or that it does. By reading that paragraph, can you tell me why it was important to pick a place that had lots of streams and rivers? What did it do for the people? How did it help them?

JENNIFER:: It gave them fresh water, fish, and a way to travel.

MAX: That it was a really smart place to settle because it was very fertile land, and then it can support lots of crops.

MR. G.: Good. So when we talk about people moving and settling for different reasons, right, we learned that the people moved here for economic reasons. And then the second key concept was how the geography influenced the people. And, as Max said, it was fertile land, so good crops would grow, and those crops would help the colony. Great. So as we were reading, we were trying to determine what's most important to remember to help us learn about our big ideas and compare this colony to the others we are reading about. Let's keep reading the next section to see if we can find any important information about how they started to govern themselves.

[The students continue reading to learn about the third big idea.]

Your Turn: Talking the Talk!

1 Select a group of students that needs help distinguishing important from trivial information when reading.

2 Use the lesson template (Appendix A) to plan your lesson, thinking about the language choices you should make to help students understand and use the strategy of determining importance to facilitate understanding.

◆ Talk the talk! Plan how you will connect this strategy work to the students' reading goals. Pay special attention to how you will explain and model how to determine important information.

◆ Plan how you will guide the students in practice. Select passages that exemplify meaningful places to apply the strategic action. As you guide students, emphasize *how* to use the features and structure of the text to focus on what is most important.

◆ After teaching the lesson, reflect on the explicitness and clarity of your talk (Appendix B). How did it go? Did you use your talk to help students set goals, to explain and prompt students to determine important information based on those goals? Did you provide feedback that facilitated students' understanding of the text and use of determining importance? Appendix C provides three examples of teachers' responses to the reflection questions.

Lesson Plan 6: Determining What's Important

Common Core State Standard

◆ Informational Text Standard 3: Explain events, procedures, ideas, or concepts in a historical, scientific, or technical text, including what happened and why, based on specific information in the text.

Text

◆ *Pennsylvania*, National Geographic Reading Expeditions

Set the Knowledge Goals

◆ Use strategies for focusing on important information to acquire the knowledge to answer the following questions: Why did people move to the North American colonies? How did the geography and people influence life in the colonies? How did the colonies govern themselves?

Explain

1 Explain that students will use the text's structure and relevant features to focus on the most important information to answer their key questions about the North American colonies.

2 Explain that the text is divided into two sections: the history of Pennsylvania and William Penn, and that they can use the headings to help them focus on what will be most important in each section.

Guide Practice

1 Prompt students to read the first section of the text, focusing their attention on any information that is important to understanding the three knowledge goal questions. The teacher guides practice with statements such as the following:

- Prompting statements: "What have we learned in this section that relates to any of our three key questions?"

- Elaborative statements: "Can you say more about that fact?"

- Clarifying statements: "That's interesting information. How can the heading help you know what this section is mostly about?"

2 Prompt students to read the second section, again focusing their attention on the three knowledge goal questions.

3 Prompt students to record their new answers to these questions on the comparison chart of the North American colonies (using the template in Form 6.1 at the end of this chapter).

Recap and Reflect

- Remind students that focusing their attention on what is most important in an informational text can help them attain their goals for reading more efficiently. Prompt them to share how their new understanding about Pennsylvania compares to their previous understanding about the Massachusetts colony (using Form 6.1).

Colony Comparison Chart

Name(s) _____

Colonies	Why did people move to the colonies?	How did the geography and people influence life in the colonies?	How did the colonies govern themselves?
Middle			
New England			
Southern			

Making Predictions

What Is It?

Predicting is the ability to anticipate what one will read. To make a prediction about story events or information that will be learned, skilled readers use what they already know about a text's structure and meaning, and they combine this with their own background knowledge to think about what will happen next.

Why Is It Important?

Making meaning is an active process; that is, skilled readers do not just decode the words and wait for understanding to come to them (Duffy, 2009; Lipson & Wixson, 2009; Pressley, 2006). Instead, they continually monitor their understanding and anticipate what they will be reading about next. Predicting while reading has been shown to increase interest in reading (Duke & Pearson, 2002) and to have a positive impact on comprehension (Shanahan et al., 2002). However, Duke and Pearson (2010) noted that making predictions supported comprehension and learning "only if the predictions were explicitly compared to text ideas during further reading" (p. 213) and cautioned that the "verification process, in which knowledge and text are compared explicitly, may be as important as making the prediction" (p. 213–214).

When Do I Teach It?

Students do not seem to approach the text in a meaningful or purposeful way, and as they read, they do not seem to anticipate what might come next or to monitor their understanding. When they are asked to predict what they might read about next, they provide no response. In addition, when the students are asked about the accuracy of predictions already made, they either provide no response or an inaccurate response.

What Do I Do?

Select an Appropriate Text.

Prediction is a strategy good readers use as they read every text, in essence "getting their minds ready to read" by anticipating the type of information the author will share in an expository text, or, alternatively, by anticipating the actions or events that will occur in a narrative text. As such, almost any text is suitable or appropriate for teaching students to make predictions.

Set a Knowledge Goal.

Understand how and when to make and monitor predictions that will support reading engagement and contribute to text understanding.

Use Talk to Explain, Model, and Guide.

- Describe why and when students should predict when reading.
- Explain and show how to predict and to revise predictions, as needed, using clues provided in the text (e.g., pictures, title, monitoring what has happened so far). Emphasize the importance of using prediction strategies to help students focus on important ideas in the text and to help them think about and achieve their knowledge goals.
- Use explanatory talk to guide students as they predict and confirm those predictions when reading.
- Notice and name (Johnston, 2004) the strategies students use when reading and describe how those actions are facilitating their meaning making.

Recap and Reflect.

Remind students that, as they read this text, predicting will help them to check their understanding of the story and begin to think like the characters think.

Example: Putting the Plan into Practice

In the following lesson excerpt, Ms. Walsh is working one on one with Alice, a third-grade student. During the previous lessons, Ms. Walsh had been working with the class on making predictions. She noticed, however, that Alice had not volunteered any predictions during previous lessons, and she decided to create a few opportunities to work with Alice individually on this strategy. The text they are reading is from the Kate DiCamillo series, *Mercy Watson*. As you read the transcript, notice how Ms. Walsh prompts Alice to share her understanding of predicting from the previous lessons and clarifies as needed with explanatory talk about conditional strategy knowledge. Then, notice how Ms. Walsh prompts Alice to engage in predicting, offering feedback that explicitly notices the actions Alice was using, while also prompting her to elaborate on her understanding of the story and its anticipated plot.

Ms. W.: Can you remind me of what we talked about yesterday? What do good readers do before they start reading? What should we do as readers before we start reading this book, *Mercy Watson Goes for a Ride*?

Alice: Predictions.

Ms. W.: We are going to make predictions. Exactly. Why is that a good strategy for us to use when reading?

Alice: Because it's a storybook.

Ms. W.: OK. We do make predictions when we read stories, but why do we? Do you remember what we said yesterday?

Alice: Not exactly.

Ms. W.: I told you yesterday that readers make predictions because they anticipate what is going to happen and that keeps them really engaged in what they are reading. Predicting helps readers to make sure they understand what they are reading, and it also helps readers to think like the characters think. So, what do we do to make predictions?

Alice: (*looking at the good readers chart* [see Figure 7.1]) Browse.

Ms. W.: We're going to browse. I love that you referenced the chart on the wall to help you. And what do we do when we browse?

Alice: Look at the title.

Ms. W.: Mm-hmm.

Alice: And the cover and the pictures.

Ms. W.: Exactly. And then after we browse, we're ready to make predictions. And what do we use to help us make predictions?

Alice: The pictures and the title.

Ms. W.: Right. We browse through the title, cover, and pictures, and then the pictures and the title can give us an idea of what might be happening in the story.

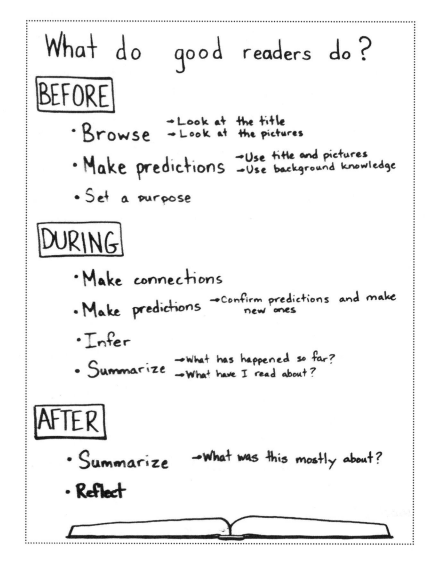

FIGURE 7.1. Ms. W.'s good readers chart.

So, let's do it. As you're doing your browsing, I want you to tell me what you're thinking and noticing.

ALICE: I noticed something like how he was dreaming that he was driving in a fast car. It came true.

MS. W.: So you're making a connection back to the first book.

ALICE: Mm-hmm.

MS. W.: That is another very smart thing that readers do to help them predict what might happen in a story. They make connections to other books they have read that are similar or in the same series. So, you think that in this book Mr. Watson's dream is going to come true. That makes sense based on what we see on the cover here. So, just like we did on our chart paper for our last story, this time we are going to record and confirm our predictions in our notebook, because readers don't only make predictions before they start a book, they are also always confirming or discomfirming and then repredicting—making new predictions—as they read to help them really focus on the story and what's happening. So, we are going to have two columns, a column for our predictions and a smaller column for when we confirm (see Figure 7.2). That first prediction you just made was fantastic. Can you restate that prediction so that we can write it down? What did you predict just by looking at the cover?

ALICE: That Mr. Watson's dream is coming true.

MS. W.: Can you say more about that?

ALICE: He had a dream about driving a fast car with no hands.

MS. W.: Great. Let's record that whole prediction in your notebook.

ALICE: (*Writes in notebook.*)

MS. W.: So, now what are you going to do?

ALICE: Browse through the pictures. (*browsing*) I predict that the policemen are going to pull over Mercy and Mr. Watson.

MS. W.: So, you were able to use the pictures to predict what might happen later in the story. Let's read to see if these predictions are confirmed or not. If you read something that makes you think they will be confirmed, let me know.

ALICE: (*reading silently*) Wait, Mercy is not getting out of the driver's seat.

MS. W.: What does that make you think?

ALICE: I thought she was going to drive the car. Then I looked at the cover again and saw Mr. Watson there.

MS. W.: Do you think Mercy's going to end up driving the car?

ALICE: Pretty much, no.

MS. W.: No. Why?

ALICE: She'd crash into a trashcan, crash into a fence.

MS. W.: Yeah, I don't think a pig driving would be very safe. Can we confirm our prediction that Mr. Watson was going to drive fast yet?

ALICE: Not yet.

MS. W.: Let's keep reading.

ALICE: (*reading silently*) Oh, here he is driving fast. You can see in the picture how everything is blowing back. And Mr. Watson likes driving like this.

MS. W.: So, you were able to confirm your first prediction based on what you have read and what you see in the picture here. Great. Are you still thinking that the policemen are going to pull them over?

ALICE: Yep.

MS. W.: Let's find out what will happen next.

ALICE: (*Continues reading silently to confirm predictions.*)

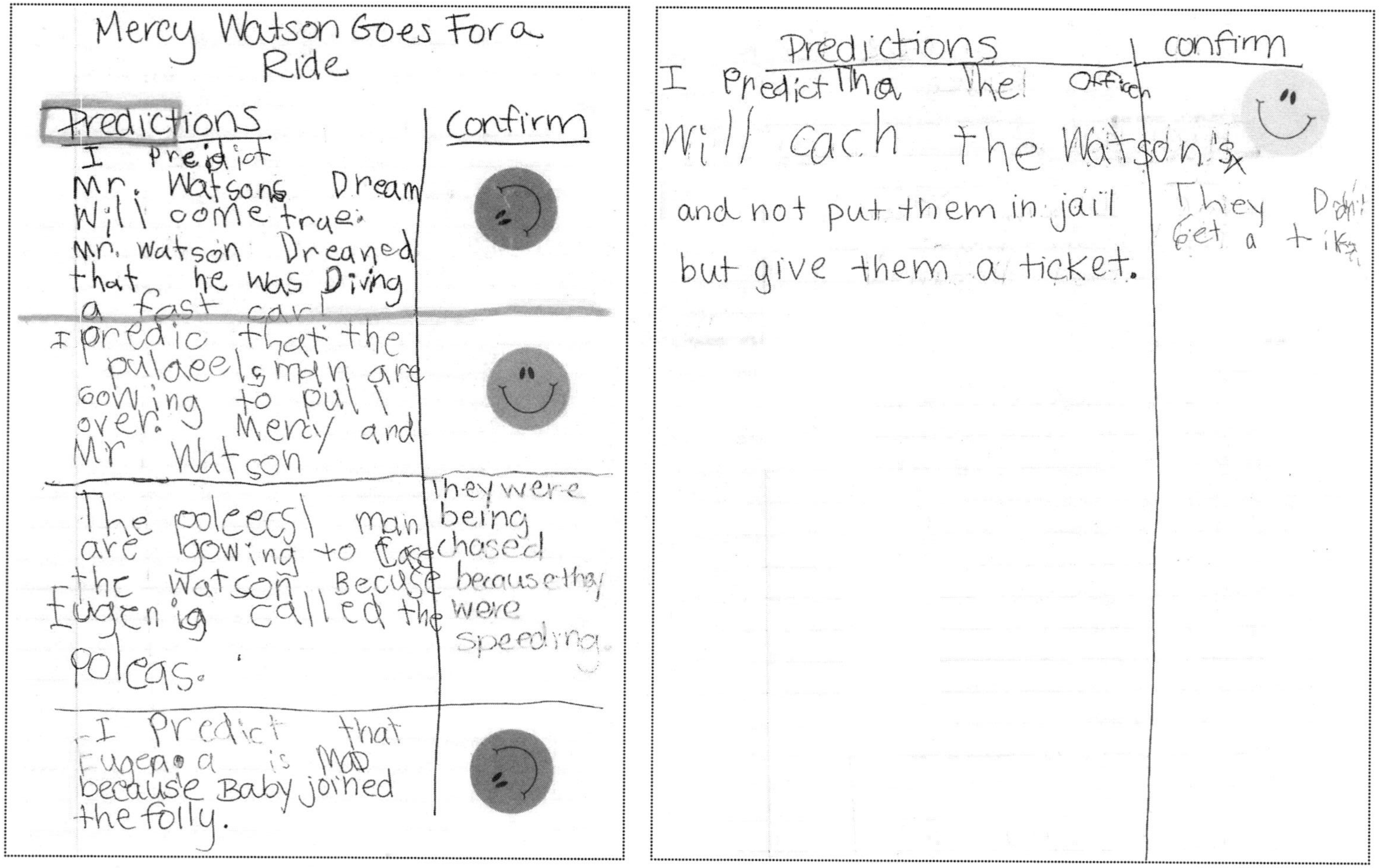

Mercy Watson Goes For a Ride

Predictions	Confirm
I predict Mr. Watsons Dream Will come true. Mr. watson Dreamed that he was Diving a fast car	☺
I predeic that the poliee is man are Going to pull over Mercy and MR Watson	☺
The poleecl man are Going to fake chased the Watson Becuse Eugenig Called the poleas.	they were being chased becausethy were speeeving ☺
I Predict that Eugena is mad because Baby joined the folly.	☺

Predictions | confirm
I predict tha the Office Will cach the Watsons and not put them in jail but give them a ticket. | ☺ They Dont get a tiket

FIGURE 7.2. Two-column chart for prediction confirmation for *Mercy Watson Goes for a Ride*, by Kate DiCamillo.

Your Turn: Talking the Talk!

1 Select a group of students who do not seem to be actively predicting when reading.

2 Use the lesson template (Appendix A) to plan your lesson, thinking about the language choices you should make to help students understand and use predicting as a strategy to facilitate understanding.

- ◆ Talk the talk! Plan how you will connect this strategy work to the students' reading goals. Pay special attention to how you will explain and model predicting.

- ◆ Plan how you will guide the students in practice. Select appropriate stopping points throughout the text that provide clues to confirming or disconfirming predictions and then repredicting. As you guide students, emphasize *how* to predict when reading. What clues are provided that lead the reader to predict?

- ◆ After teaching the lesson, reflect on the explicitness and clarity of your talk (Appendix B). How did it go? Did you use your talk to help students set goals, to explain and prompt students to predict, confirm or disconfirm, and repredict? Did you provide feedback that facilitated students' understanding of the text and of predicting as a strategy to support understanding? Appendix C provides three examples of teachers' responses to the reflection questions.

Lesson Plan 7: Making Predictions

Common Core State Standard

- ◆ Literature Standard 3: Describe characters in a story (e.g., their traits, motivations, or feelings) and explain how their actions contribute to the sequence of events.
- ◆ Literature Standard 7: Explain how specific aspects of a text's illustrations contribute to what is conveyed by the words in a story (e.g., create mood, emphasize aspects of a character or setting).

Text

- ◆ *Mercy Watson Goes for a Ride*, by Kate DiCamillo (Geisel Award Honor Book)

Set the Knowledge Goal

- ◆ Use prediction strategies before and during reading to understand and clarify story events by anticipating what will happen next and staying engaged while reading.

Explain

1 Explain that students will make predictions about the text by first browsing through the story, examining the title, cover, and illustrations.

2 Explain that making predictions about this text will help students stay involved in their reading by helping them to check their understanding and think like the characters think.

Guide Practice

1 Prompt students to browse through the book, noticing the title, cover illustration, and illustrations throughout the text. Guide the students' predicting with statements such as the following:

- Prompting statements: "What do you predict will happen from looking at the cover? What are the illustrations throughout the text making you think?"

- Elaborative statements: "Why are you thinking that? What makes you think that will happen? Can you say more about that?"

2 Prompt students to record their predictions in their notebook using the two-column template in Form 7.1 at the end of this chapter. The teacher provides facilitative feedback statements, such as the following:

- Feedback statements: "You made that prediction using the cover and title for the book. Doing that will help you make logical predictions."

3 Prompt students to read to confirm initial predictions or revise predictions as needed, based on what has happened in the text. Guide students with further elaborative and clarifying statements and facilitative feedback.

Recap and Reflect

- Remind students that predicting while reading will help them to stay focused on the text. As they read this story, predicting will help them to understand the characters and events by anticipating what might happen next. Checking and either confirming or revising their predictions will help them understand what is happening and will also help them make new predictions.

Two-Column Chart for Prediction Confirmation

Name _____

Title _____ Author _____

Prediction	Confirmed?

Making Connections

What Is It?

Skilled readers make connections between the words and ideas in the text they are reading and their own lives. These connections might be to their own experiences, knowledge they have of the world around them, or to other books or media they have accessed.

Why Is It Important?

When skilled readers make connections to texts by comparing and contrasting their own experiences and prior knowledge with the ideas in the texts, they are more likely to understand and remember what they have read (Dole, Brown, & Trathen, 1996; Pressley, 2006). Moreover, when readers do not think about connections to the texts they read, they are less likely to appropriately or accurately employ other strategic actions, such as inferring and visualizing, both of which help texts come alive (Duffy, 2009). As we consider instructional strategies that support students' ability to make connections, we must be particularly mindful of two important research findings. The first is that making connections is dependent on having a *relevant* store of knowledge or experience (Beck, Omanson, & McKeown, 1982)— quite obviously a reader cannot make a connection to a topic or an idea about which nothing is known! The second, however, is that having relevant knowledge will not, by itself, ensure that readers will use it to make connections. That is, the process of making connections to support comprehension is not necessarily automatic or intuitive during the act of reading—sometimes readers fail to *use* what they know to make sense of a text (Hansen, 1981). Like other reading strategies, students must be taught how, when, and why making connections will deepen their understanding of text.

When Do I Teach It?

Explicitly teach students to make connections when you notice that they do not access their own experiences and background knowledge to help them understand and question what they are reading, and in turn, they are not making logical inferences.

What Do I Do?

Select an Appropriate Text.

Making connections to text is clearly an important strategy, but it is not a "fail-proof" strategy. That is, sometimes, readers can make connections that take them off-track and distract them from the author's main ideas or point of view. When preparing to teach students the strategy of making connections, then, we must think carefully about the focal text. Is it one for which meaning will be deepened and enhanced if students' relate their own background knowledge and experience? Choose the focal text carefully and deliberately, thinking about your students and their background knowledge and experiences in relation to the texts you are considering and the knowledge goals you intend to work toward.

Set a Knowledge Goal.

Begin the lesson by explaining how making connections will help students relate what they already know to the information in the text.

Use Talk to Explain, Model, and Guide.

- Access or develop background knowledge requisite for comprehending the selection.
- Describe why students should make connections when reading.
- Explain and show how to make connections that prompt deeper thinking.
- Notice and name (Johnston, 2004) the connections they make between their own knowledge and experiences and the information in the text.

Recap and Reflect.

Discuss how connecting to one's own experiences helps the reader to understand important ideas in the text.

Example: Putting the Plan into Practice

In the following lesson excerpt, Ms. Michaels is working with a small group of sixth-grade students, Elizabeth, Allison, Tatyana, and Fiona. Although the students could describe what it meant to make connections, Ms. Michaels had noticed that they rarely used this strategy to help them understand the characters' motivations and feelings in the books they were reading. As you read the transcript, note that Ms. Michaels starts out by explaining why it is important to make connections when reading a book such as *Stargirl*, by Jerry Spinelli. Then, notice how she models her own thinking, involving connections and other thoughts, while also pointing out how her thinking is helping her to understand a little more about the characters.

MS. M.: We're going to start with *Stargirl* today, but we're going to go back to the very beginning and do a little rereading. Why is it important to do a reread?

FIONA: Because sometimes you forget if you don't read the same book in a few days—because that happened to me with my summer reading and I had to reread the whole book.

MS. M.: Right, and sometimes rereading can also help us understand more about the book we are presently reading. Rereading can help us recall important information or sometimes clarify information for us. Remember, as we read today we are thinking about what it really means to fit in, and as we reread these first chapters, we're going to work on making connections between our own experiences and the characters in the text to help us understand this idea of fitting in. Do any of you know anything about making connections to the books you are reading?

ELIZABETH: It helps you relate to the story.

MS. M.: Can you tell me a little bit about what you mean by *relate to the story?*

ELIZABETH: If you have . . . if the character that is in the book does something or thinks something that you have done before, and then you think, "Oh, that has happened to me before," you relate to them.

MS. M.: Good, that's absolutely correct. It also helps us think about or sort of get inside the character's head to figure out what the character might be thinking or why he or she might be doing the things that he or she is doing. And it can help us also with our predictions because if we think about how we acted in a situation, it can help us predict how the character might act in a situation. Does that make sense?

ALL: Yes.

MS. M.: Now with our book, *Stargirl*, why do you think focusing on making connections to the text would help us understand the story a bit better? What is it about *Stargirl*? There are a lot characters in the story, so there are many opportunities for us to relate to the characters and understand their motivations and actions, depending on our personality and our experiences. Also, since the genre is realistic fiction, there are going to be a lot of experiences that I think we have all gone through and can comment on. Now, as we are making connections to *Stargirl* today, I want you to keep in mind that sometimes our connections are unproductive. They don't really help us to understand the characters and the story; they are just kind of related to what happened. So you want to make sure that your connections are productive, meaning, they connect very closely to the story. Keeping our connections very focused and "on topic" helps us understand the story a little more and helps us to think more deeply about the text. Fair enough?

ELIZABETH: Mm-hmm.

MS. M.: OK, so let's get started. I want to show you how I might make connections as I read so you'll know what I mean by *productive connections* that help us understand the story more. Then you'll have an opportunity to try it in Chapter Two. Just because we're focusing on making connections, however, does not mean that you should forget other strategies we have worked on. If you want to stop and ask questions and make predictions and clarify your reading, you should do that.

(*Reads aloud. In this part of the chapter, the narrator explains that at age 12, he moved from Pennsylvania to Arizona. Ms. M. then stops reading and thinks aloud.*) I moved only once in my life and I remember, when I moved from my house that I grew up in to a different house, feeling very sad. I wonder if the narrator was sad to move to Arizona.

(*Continues reading: "At the time, I simply considered the episode a mystery. It did not occur to me that I was being watched. We were all being watched."*)

(*Thinks aloud.*) So, at the end, where those two sentences repeat a little there, that gives me a little bit of a freaked-out feeling. Who's watching them?

(*Continues reading aloud: "In the front of Science I heard a name: Stargirl. I turned to the senior slouching behind me. 'Stargirl,' I said, 'what kind of name is that?' 'That's it, Stargirl Carroway. She said it in homeroom.' 'Stargirl?' 'Yeah.' And then I saw her at lunch. She wore an off-white dress so long it covered her shoes. It had ruffles around the necks and cuffs and looked like it could've been her great grandmother's wedding gown. Her hair was the color of sand, it fell to her shoulders. Something was strapped across her back but it wasn't a book bag. At first I thought it was a miniature guitar; I found out later it was a ukulele. She did not carry a lunch-tray. I never got lunch either. She did carry a large canvas bag with a life-size sunflower painted on it. The lunch room was dead silent as she walked by."*)

(*Thinks aloud.*) I think that that's probably because they're stunned by her outfit and her "not-fitting-in-ness." I remember seeing people in my high school who didn't look like the other kids. Everyone seemed to notice them. I wonder if this is making Stargirl feel a little self-conscious.

(*Resumes her "teaching voice."*) So again, I have been trying to make connections between my prior experiences and what was happening to the characters in the story. When I was doing this, I was thinking more about the characters and how they were feeling. OK, I'm going to stop there, and I'm going to have you all pick up where I left off. Remember, I want you to think about the connections you can make to what is happening with the characters. I want you to note your connections on sticky notes [see Figure 8.1 for Ms. M.'s example] just as I have been doing here. OK?

[The lesson continues with students reading silently and noting connections while Ms. Michaels confers with individual students.]

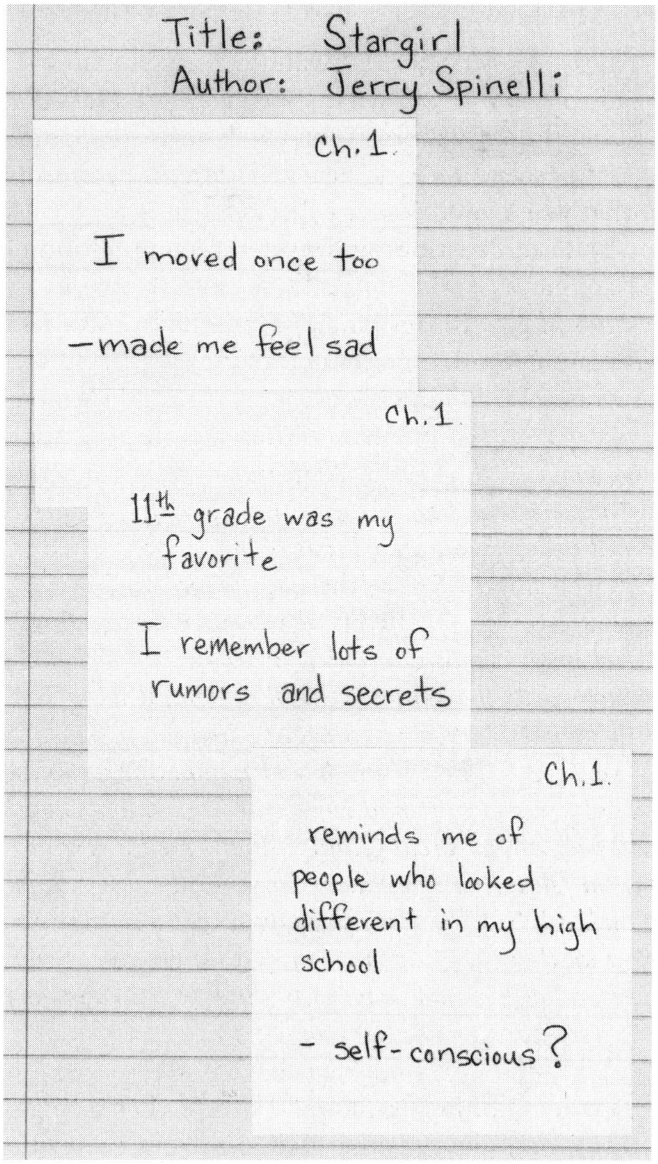

Title: Stargirl
Author: Jerry Spinelli

Ch. 1

I moved once too

—made me feel sad

Ch. 1

11th grade was my favorite

I remember lots of rumors and secrets

Ch. 1

reminds me of people who looked different in my high school

— self-conscious?

FIGURE 8.1. Using sticky notes to record connections.

Your Turn: Talking the Talk!

1 Select a group of students that needs help understanding the importance of connecting the texts they read to their own experiences and background knowledge.

2 Use the lesson template (Appendix A) to plan your lesson, thinking about the language choices you should make to help students understand and use making connections as a strategy to facilitate understanding.

◆ Talk the talk! Plan how will you relate the emphasis on making connections to the students' knowledge goals for the lesson. Throughout your lesson planning, pay special attention to how you will explain and model making connections.

◆ Plan how you will guide the students as they practice making connections between the text and their own knowledge and experiences. Select phrases, lines, and passages that exemplify meaningful places for students to stop and make connections to their own lives. As you guide students, emphasize *how* to connect to the text and *how* those connections help them infer how the characters are feeling and what is motivating them to act in certain ways.

◆ After teaching the lesson, reflect on the explicitness and clarity of your talk (Appendix B). How did it go? Did you use your talk to help students set goals, to explain and prompt students to make connections while reading? Did you provide feedback that facilitated students' understanding of how making connections will help them as readers? Appendix C provides three examples of teachers' responses to the reflection questions.

Lesson Plan 8: Making Connections

Common Core State Standard

◆ Literature Standard 1: Cite textual evidence to support analysis of what the text says explicitly as well as inferences drawn from the text.

◆ Literature Standard 3: Describe how a particular story's or drama's plot unfolds in a series of episodes as well as how the characters respond or change as the plot moves toward a resolution.

Text

◆ *Stargirl*, by Jerry Spinelli

Set the Knowledge Goal

1 How does making connections between our own prior experiences and background knowledge deepen our understanding of characters and their relationships?

2 Is it important to always fit in with a group? Why or why not?

Explain

1 Explain that students will be making connections between their own experiences and those of the characters in the story to help them gain a deeper understanding of the characters and their motives and actions.

2 Explain why making connections is a strategy particularly suited to this type of text. (The text's plot and the knowledge goal chosen for these students are both within the realm of their own school and life experiences.)

3 Model how to make connections to the text and how those connections lead the reader to think more about why a character is acting in a certain way or how a character might be feeling.

Guide Practice

1 Prompt students to make connections to the characters as they continue reading on their own. Have the students record their connections on sticky notes.

- Prompting statements: "What does this part remind you of? Has anything like this happened to you before? How did that make you feel? What did you do?"

- Elaborative statements: "Can you say more about that?"

- Clarifying statements: "How is that connection helping you to understand the character more? Can you show me what made you think that?"

2 Prompt students to share their connections and subsequent new understandings about the characters.

3 Prompt students to reflect on how these connections have helped them to think about the importance of fitting in with a group.

Recap and Reflect

- Remind students that making connections helps readers to remember and learn from text because they are relating what is happening in the text to the experiences they have had or have heard about. In this story, making connections helps students make inferences about the characters that help deepen their understanding of the text.

Summarizing

What Is It?

Summarizing is the process of concisely describing the main points of a text either orally or in writing. To summarize, readers must be able to first determine what information in the text is important, and then they must be able to convey the information accurately and succinctly in their own words (Dole, Duffy, Roehler, & Pearson, 1991).

Why Is It Important?

Summarizing during and after reading will help students to remember and learn information that they have read. There is strong evidence that engaging in summarization, in conjunction with other comprehension strategies, can help students overcome difficulties in comprehension, compensate for incomplete background knowledge, and learn to organize their thinking about texts around the internal structures within which they are written (Duke & Pearson, 2002; Shanahan et al., 2010). The importance of explicitly teaching summarization (rather than simply assigning it as a task for students to complete after reading) is underscored by evidence that many students are unable to produce summaries on their own, and, furthermore, that summarizing is especially difficult for poorer readers (Brown & Day, 1983; McGee, 1982). However, when students of all ability levels are taught sound strategies for summarizing (e.g., explicit instruction on procedures for summarizing, using increasingly longer and more difficult passages), their comprehension improves both on the text at hand and on other texts, as measured by standardized testing (Armbruster, Anderson, & Ostertag, 1987; Duke & Pearson, 2002). Low-performing students are likely to need more practice and more facilitative feedback than their higher-performing peers (Armbruster et al., 1987).

When Do I Teach It?

Explicitly teach summarization strategies when you observe that students are not able to identify important information in text and report it in their own words, or, when asked to summarize, they typically include unimportant information, may omit important information, and/or tell everything that they read in the text.

What Do I Do?

Select a Procedure for Summarizing.

Effective instruction of summarization is based on explanation and modeling of a clear set of rules or procedures that teach students how to accurately identify important ideas in the text and how to coherently represent the information they selected. The central idea that must guide students as they work toward summarization, especially when they are reading long and complex text, is having a clear understanding of *what to keep and what to throw away*. Although there are different approaches to summarization (Duke & Pearson, 2002), one approach that has proven successful in improving students' ability to compose an accurate and coherent summary and in improving students' overall comprehension is the instruction of "rules for summarization" (Brown & Day, 1983; McNeil & Donant, 1982; Bean & Steenwyk, 1984). The rules are as follows:

♦ *Rule 1. Delete unnecessary material.* Direct students to consider the main ideas in the selection. Text structure may be helpful in teaching this idea. That is, in a story, reporting the key elements of the setting, problem, solution, and consequence is important. In expository prose, thinking about the writer's plan or structure (e.g., cause–effect, comparison, consequence, time order) may be a useful way to consider the important ideas. Only ideas that are central to the structure, then, are included. This rule helps students distinguish between "interesting" ideas (e.g., the colors a character wears) and important ideas (e.g., ideas central to the selection's structure).

♦ *Rule 2. Delete redundant material.* Have students reread and attend to repetition of ideas. Have them delete ideas that are stated more than once.

♦ *Rule 3. Substitute a superordinate term for a list of items.* To follow this rule, guide students to think about the ideas that can be generalized and represented by a single term. For example, in a selection in which a character has a dog, a cat, a fish, and a gerbil, one could superordinate by using the words *many pets*.

◆ *Rule 4. Compose a superordinate term to represent the individual parts of an action.* Similar to rule 3, to follow this rule, guide students to think about ideas that can be superordinated or generalized with a word or phrase. For example, in a selection about farming in Australia, a statement that "In Australia regions of the country vary widely in climate condition and, as a result, crops differ by region" could superordinate detailed information about the specific crops raised in the north, south, east, and west.

◆ *Rule 5. Select or invent a topic sentence.* Explain that good summaries include an explicit statement that tells the main idea of the selection. Sometimes students can find this in the text. Other times they must invent or think of it themselves. Depending on the selection and the students' familiarity with summarization, you might work on these rules over time. For example, you might begin by working with small segments of text, learning to identify and report important ideas in a concise manner, and in later lessons progress to working with longer and more complex segments of text. Throughout the process, summarization is typically used in conjunction with other reading strategies (e.g., visualizing, making inferences or making connections to clarify meaning).

Set a Knowledge Goal.

Begin the lesson by establishing how summarizing during and after reading will help students reach their goals of understanding and learning from what they read.

Use Talk to Explain, Model, and Guide.

- ◆ Describe why summarizing is a useful strategy to employ to monitor understanding and remember key ideas.

- ◆ Explain and show how to use the structure and features of a text to determine what is most important to remember. Then show how to restate those main points in one's own words.

- ◆ Use explanatory talk to guide students as they use a text's structure and features to summarize sections that they have read. Guide students as they combine their ongoing summaries into a summary of the whole text.

- ◆ Notice and name (Johnston, 2004) the summarizing actions students are using well and describe how those actions are helping them to learn and remember what they have read.

Recap and Reflect.

Restate and discuss the importance of summarizing as a tool to enhance understanding and learning from text because it helps the reader to organize information coherently around a logical structure.

Example: Putting the Plan into Practice

In the following lesson excerpt, Ms. Bates is working with a group of three second-grade students, Vincent, Luis, and Raphael. The class has been doing research on wild animals, and this group had chosen tigers as their topic. The group is reading *Endangered Tigers*, by Bobbie Kalman, and Ms. Bates has chosen to teach the students how to summarize while reading to answer the questions they generated prior to reading. As you read the transcript, notice how Ms. Bates explains and models how to use the headings in the text as a way to determine whether information is important or not. Then, notice how she guides them through a section of text, offering clarification and cues to focus their attention when the students are hesitant to respond or incorrect in their attempts to use the strategy.

Ms. B.: OK, we have been researching wild animals to understand more about the characteristics—remember, that word means what they look like and sometimes how they act—of different animals, how they live in their habitats, and how they adapt to their surroundings. You guys all started to do research about tigers last time, and you generated a whole bunch of questions that you wanted to know more about. Are you ready? Look up at our chart so that we can all read them.

Students: (*chorally reading*) Can tigers go in water? What do tigers eat? Where do they live?

Ms. B.: OK.

Students: (*chorally reading*) What do tigers look like? How do they jump? How do tiger cubs eat? Why do tigers go through bushes? Where do they find food? Why do tigers go in grass?

Ms. B.: OK. Today we're going to continue to read our text, *Endangered Tigers*, together to see if we can find any of the answers to the questions that we asked. OK? Let's see, yesterday we read the sections "Tigers Are Endangered" and "Five Living Tigers," and we learned about tigers being endangered, which means that some are at risk of dying out, and we learned about the different types of tigers and how some are already extinct. Let's use the table of contents to see what section is next. (*prompting students to turn to the table of contents page*) What is the next section, Luis?

Luis: (*reading*) "Tigers Are M—"

Ms. B.: Let's look at the word. *Mammals.* Now we're going to be reading "Tigers Are Mammals." Can you all read that section title?

Students: (*reading*) "Tigers Are Mammals."

Ms. B.: Great. "Tigers Are Mammals." As we read this section we are going to continue to use summarizing as a strategy to help us learn and remember the information we are reading about tigers, just like we did yesterday. And so when we turn to that page, we can see that those same words are at the top of the page.

Those words are called a *heading*. Do you remember that from yesterday? We're going to look at the headings as we read, and the headings are going to help us predict the information that we're going to be reading about tigers. And then we can use the headings to help us summarize the information. Remember that when we summarize, we are deciding what information is important to remember and then trying to say that information back in our own words. When we do that, we are more likely to remember what we have just read. So (*reading*) "Tigers Are Mammals." What is this page going to be all about?

STUDENTS: (*no response*)

MS. B.: Since it says *tigers are mammals*, I know that this page is going to be all about them being mammals, but if I'm not quite sure what a *mammal* is, I'm going to be able to read this and find out. So as we summarize, we're going to figure out the important information and then we can retell it in our own words, and the important information is going to be about tigers being mammals just like the heading says. Let me show you.

(*reading*) "Tigers are mammals. All mammals are warm-blooded. Their bodies stay the same temperature no matter how hot or cold the air or water around them is." So mammals' bodies always stay the same temperature. (*reading*) "Baby mammals drink milk from their mothers' bodies."

OK, let me summarize what's going on here so far, because I want to make sure this is making sense to me. I have my heading "Tigers Are Mammals," so I know I'm learning about what?

VINCENT: Mammals.

MS. B.: OK, but what are mammals? Let me summarize. Tigers are mammals. Mammals are warm-blooded, and they also . . . what does *warm-blooded* mean? (*reading from text*) "Their bodies stay the same temperature." Oh, I know my body always stays at 98.6 degrees. You know how when you get the thermometer and you're seeing what your temperature is? Do you know how you do that? And my body's always the same, but I also know that snakes, though, they always have a different temperature. If it's hot, their body temperature is hot, but if it's cold, it's cold. And I also noticed something else, that the baby mammals drink from their mother's body. So what do the baby cubs eat?

LUIS: Milk.

MS. B.: Yeah, and where does that milk come from, Raphael?

RAPHAEL: Their mothers.

MS. B.: Milk from their mothers. Good. So now I can summarize. I use my heading and I have "mammals are warm-blooded and they also drink milk from their mother's bodies." I can summarize the important information about that heading and I know . . . I can understand what I just read.

Let's try it with this next part. Let's read. Where's the heading, Vincent?

VINCENT: Heading?

MS. B.: Yeah, where's the heading on that page?

VINCENT: (*Points to heading.*)

MS. B.: Yeah. What does that say?

VINCENT: (*reading*) "Striped Coats."

MS. B.: So that's probably going to be about them having . . .

LUIS: Striped coats.

MS. B.: Striped coats. Let's read this next part in our heads and find out. (*reading silently*) I know mammals are warm-blooded and that they drink milk from their mothers, and now in this section on striped coats, what have we learned about tigers?

RAPHAEL: They have hair.

MS. B.: OK, it did say they have hair. Can we say more about that? Does someone have something they can add?

RAPHAEL: Their coats have hair or fur.

MS. B.: Right, that gives us a little more information. Does that information make sense for the heading "Striped Coats"?

STUDENTS: Yeah.

MS. B.: Yes, it does, so that is important to remember. Anything else that was important?

VINCENT: They have a backbone.

MS. B.: Hmm. It's true that they have a backbone. I wonder if that is going to be important to summarize in this section on "Striped Coats" because their backbone is inside their bodies, like our bones are inside, but their coat is on the outside, right?

LUIS: Oh, yeah, so I don't think so.

MS. B.: Is there any other important information that we read related to striped coats?

STUDENTS: (*no response*)

MS. B.: Hmm. I know they have hair or fur. Let's reread to check. (*reading*) "They also have hair or fur on their bodies. All tigers have beautiful fur coats. Most tigers are orange with dark stripes but a few have no stripes at all." Any other important information?

VINCENT: They are orange with dark stripes.

MS. B.: Oh. Does that match our heading?

LUIS: Yeah.

MS. B.: Yeah, it does. Do you think that should be considered important information?

LUIS: Yes.

MS. B.: Say more, Luis. Yes . . . because?

LUIS: Because it tells about the stripes—like what color they are and stuff.

MS. B.: Exactly. So now, let's think about how we might summarize in our own words what we just read about striped coats.

RAPHAEL: Tigers have hair and fur and usually it is orange with stripes.

VINCENT: Orange with dark stripes.

MS. B.: I like how Raphael said both of those important ideas we were just reading about, and I also like how Vincent clarified one of the details to make it a little more specific. Did that sound like it summarized all of the information we've read, Luis?

LUIS: Yeah.

MS. B.: Yeah, I think it does, too. So now let's think. Does that answer one of our questions we have up there? (*reading from chart*) "Where do tigers live? What do tigers look like?"

RAPHAEL: What do they look like?

MS. B.: Yeah, so we can go back and answer that question using the summary we have just said. (*Writes summary on chart under question* [see Figure 9.1].) Great. Let's keep going to the next section.

[The lesson continues with guided practice of one more text section.]

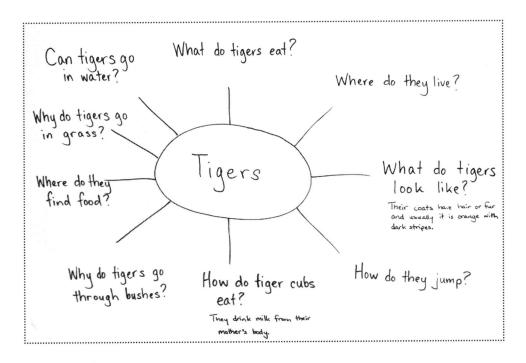

FIGURE 9.1. Summary web for tiger research.

Your Turn: Talking the Talk!

1 Select a group of students that needs help understanding and using summarizing as a strategy to support comprehension.

2 Use the lesson template (Appendix A) to plan your lesson, thinking about the language choices you should make to help students summarize during and after reading.

- ◆ Talk the talk! Plan how you will connect this strategy work to the students' reading goals. Pay special attention to how you will explain and model summarizing.

- ◆ Plan how you will guide the students in practice. Select passages or text features (e.g., headings) that exemplify meaningful places to apply the strategic action. As you guide students, emphasize *how* to summarize the text and *how* the text's overall organization facilitates their ability to summarize.

- ◆ After teaching the lesson, reflect on the explicitness and clarity of your talk (Appendix B). How did it go? Did you use your talk to help students set goals, to explain and prompt students to summarize during and after reading? Did you provide feedback that facilitated students' understanding of how summarizing will help them as readers? Appendix C provides three examples of teachers' responses to the reflection questions.

Lesson Plan 9: Summarizing

Common Core State Standard

- ◆ Informational Text Standard 1: Ask and answer such questions as who, what, where, when, why, and how to demonstrate understanding of key details in a text.
- ◆ Informational Text Standard 2: Identify the main topic of a multiparagraph text as well as the focus of specific paragraphs within the text.

Text

- ◆ *Endangered Tigers*, by Bobbie Kalman

Set the Knowledge Goal

- ◆ To differentiate between "interesting" and "important" ideas and support understanding and recall of important information about tigers by questioning and summarizing during and after reading.

Explain

1 Explain that students will be using summarizing as a strategy to help them answer their research questions. The teacher explains how summarizing helps students focus on only the important information to remember.

2 Model how to use the headings provided in the informational text to focus their attention on whether the information they are reading would be considered important. The teacher then models how to put those important details into a concise summary.

Guide Practice

1 Prompt students to read the heading and the next section of text, paying attention to what information would be important based on the words in the heading.

◆ Prompting statements: "What did we just learn in this part? What details are the most important to remember."
◆ Clarifying statements: "Let's look back at the heading. Do you think that detail is important based on what the heading is?"

2 Prompt students to reread as needed to help them learn and remember the information.

3 Prompt students to summarize in their own words the important details that they collectively identified. Provide facilitative feedback such as the following:

◆ Feedback statements: "Good. That detail relates directly to the words in the heading, and therefore it is an important piece of information to include in our summary."

4 Prompt students to think about whether the ideas they summarized they generated answer any of their research questions. Record the students' ideas under the appropriate questions on the chart. See Form 9.1 at the end of this chapter for a blank template.

Recap and Reflect

◆ Remind students that skilled readers summarize the important information they read in texts to help them learn and remember what they have read when they are researching. Discuss what the students have learned about the characteristics of tigers or how tigers have adapted to living in their environments.

Summary Web for Research

Name(s) _____

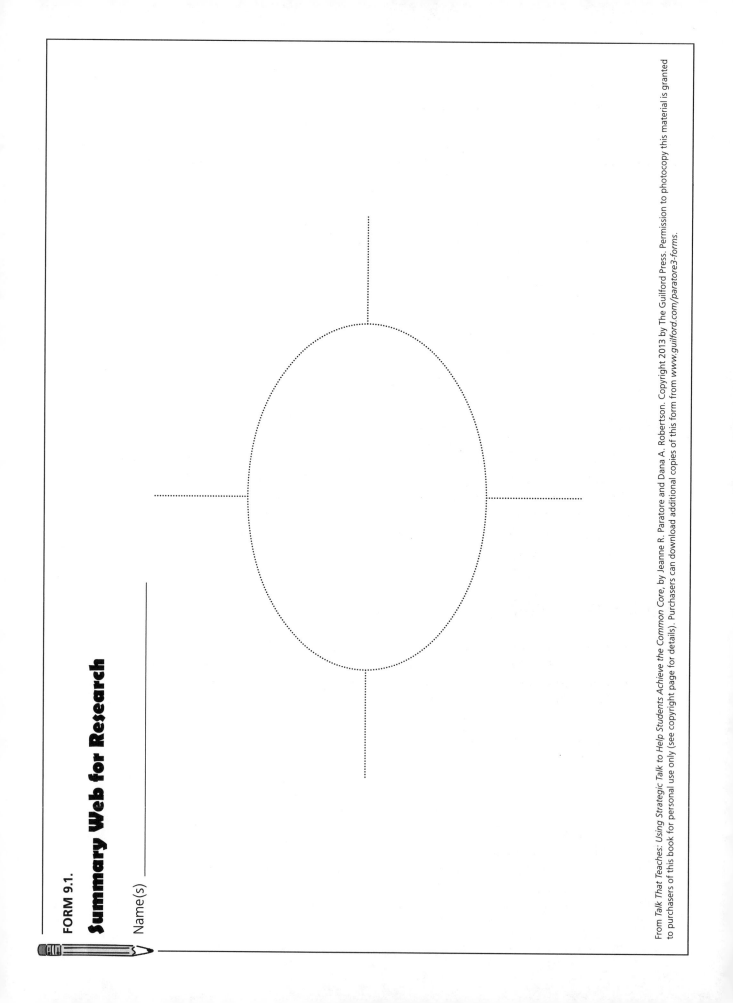

Lesson 10

Close Reading

What Is It?

When readers do close readings of texts, they slow their reading down and think carefully about the words on the page. They may try to understand why the author chose certain words. They may question what those words convey about this particular idea, and they consider implications for the overall meaning of the text. When doing close reading, or analytic reading, readers are using an array of reading strategies to piece together the meaning of the entire text.

Why Is It Important?

The CCSS that frame instruction in many schools (National Governors Association Center for Best Practices and Council of Chief State School Officers, 2010) have revived and brought to teachers' attention the need for students to be able to read complex texts closely to gain deeper understanding of the author's message. Complex texts require a reader to slow down, deliberately consider the words the author used, and consider key details so as to savor and enjoy the text while also acquiring the meaning the author was trying to convey (Newkirk, 2010). Reading in this way leads readers to question the text and consider reasonable and valid interpretations as they dig for deeper meaning, but it also requires that readers maintain interpretations that are grounded in the evidence of the text. Even though all reading does not require this level of scrutiny, we need to teach students how and when reading closely and analytically is warranted (Newkirk, 2010).

Although the emphasis on close reading and, in particular, on focusing on text-based evidence, has led some curriculum developers and classroom teachers to conclude that they should deemphasize the development of background knowledge prior to students' reading, and that they should discourage students from connecting their own experiences to the text, doing so disregards substantial evidence about practices that result in text comprehension. In the case of background knowledge, there is strong and credible evidence (Duke & Pearson, 2002; Pressley, 2006) that engagement in and comprehension of text are enhanced when readers begin with requisite background knowledge. However, we know that opportunities to develop background knowledge through rich and broad experiences vary widely among the students in our classrooms. For those who have had fewer opportunities to acquire knowledge through reading or real-world experiences, failure to develop requisite background knowledge places them at a clear disadvantage, and potentially denies them access and opportunities to learn from the required curriculum.

Making connections to relevant experiences, too, has strong research support (Hansen, 1981; Beck et al., 1982; Duke & Pearson, 2002; Pressley, 2006) as a comprehension strategy. We know that many—perhaps even most—authors compose texts with the expectation that readers will bring to bear their background knowledge and experiences to construct the full meaning of their words. To deliberately instruct students to do otherwise risks diminishing, rather than deepening, comprehension.

So, as we work to incorporate close reading into our classroom practices, we must do so without disregarding the research-based practices that ground skilled reading. That is, we must continue to build requisite background knowledge in preparation for reading, and even as we relentlessly require students to pay close attention to the evidence presented in the text, we must also remind them that, at times, making sense of what we read and critically evaluating ideas in the text requires us to consider the information in light of our background knowledge and experiences.

When Do I Teach It?

Instruction in when and how to engage in close reading is warranted when you observe that students read all texts quickly and do not demonstrate awareness of the need or ability to regulate the way they read based on their purpose or learning goals. When questioned about the text's meanings, students are only able to provide the gist or general understandings and are unable to defend or justify their ideas with evidence from the text. Students also may overrely on background knowledge to comprehend a text's message.

What Do I Do?

Select a Text and Purpose for Reading.

Close reading is a strategy we use to achieve particular reading and knowledge goals. We may use it (1) when we are reading texts that are dense with information that we must thoroughly understand and recall; (2) when we are examining texts that present a novel idea or opposing points of view; or (3) if we are examining and trying to understand a writer's craft or style. Choosing a text for close reading requires that it is a strong match for both the reading purpose (e.g., to understand alternative or opposing points of view; to describe a writer's style) and that it is sufficiently dense in concepts or stylistic interest to be worthy of close reading.

Set a Knowledge Goal.

Begin the lesson by explaining that close reading of texts will help students to think about and construct deep understanding of the author's meaning.

Use Talk to Explain, Model, and Guide.

- Describe when close reading of texts would be beneficial.
- Explain and show how to engage in close reading of text.
- Use explanatory talk as you guide students in a close reading of shared text.
- Notice and name (Johnston, 2004) strategies the students use when they are engaged in close reading and describe how those actions support deep understanding.

Recap and Reflect.

Discuss how reading texts closely will help students understand more about what the author was really trying to tell them in the text.

Example: Putting the Plan into Practice

In the following lesson excerpt, Mr. Richardson is teaching a whole-class lesson on close reading to his fifth-grade students using the text *Fly Away Home*, by Eve Bunting. Previous to this lesson, the class had been taught specific comprehension strategies (e.g., inferring, predicting, connecting), and they also had been taught to follow the narrative story structure. But Mr. Richardson had noticed that many of the students were employing these strategic actions sporadically throughout the texts they were reading. As you read the transcript, notice how Mr. Richardson first explains and models how to read *Fly Away Home* closely, thinking about all of the lines in the text. Then, after the students engaged in guided practice of the strategy, notice how Mr. Richardson recaps and reflects with the students on how close reading helped them deeply understand the texts they were reading.

MR. R.: Over the past few weeks, we have been following the narrative story structure in our books, retelling the plot, and we've also been getting to know the characters in our story by looking at their actions, their dialogue, and their thoughts. But when I'm reading, I don't just have isolated thoughts about the character. I read and I think about—the key word is *think*—critically about what I'm reading. I'm questioning answers as I'm reading, not just answering questions. And getting lost in the world of the story is not enough for me. As a reader I don't want to ever be lost when I'm reading. I want to know exactly where I am at all times. And to do this I read texts closely and accurately, because it is in these details that the questions are found. It's in these details that meaning is found, and meaning is what really matters to good readers.

When we read *Fly Away Home*, by Eve Bunting, the other day, as a community we had thoughts about the characters based on their actions, their dialogue, and their thoughts, but there is more to really understanding the story than just these thoughts. When I read *Fly Away Home* with a wide-awake mind, and I read closely and accurately, I learn more about what the author is trying to communicate and what the story really means to me.

Watch me as I show you how I jot my thinking on the two columns, just like we did yesterday. And listen for how I carry these thoughts with me as I continue in the story, because I don't want it to be an isolated thought. I want one thought to build on another thought, to build on another thought, to really put the story together.

Fly Away Home by Eve Bunting. (*Reads a line.*) What is Eve Bunting really trying to say here? I think she's trying to say that the dad and the narrator—they must be poor—they probably don't have another home judging by the fact that they're living in an airport. I wonder why they don't have a home. Is the dad not working? I wonder why they chose the airport as the place to stay. (*Writes on chart* [see Figure 10.1].)

(*Reads two lines.*) Hmm. Well, what I'm thinking here is, judging by the fact that she said, "the airport's better than the streets," it's making me think that the dad must be concerned for the son's safety. They don't have a home, and he's concerned that the son is going to be OK. (*Writes on chart* [see Figure 10.1].) This kind of reminds me of my mom, just like I was mentioning yesterday— how my mom was so concerned for my safety. Anytime I went somewhere with friends, or anytime I was riding my bike in the street, she was always saying, "Don't go here," and "Make sure you call when you get there." So, I'm kind of getting the sense, knowing how my mom would be reacting, what the dad might be going through here. I wonder how long they have been in the airport? Are there other people living there, too? Did you notice, as I'm reading this closely with those details and I read a line, it doesn't just lead me to have one thought? I can have a thought about a thought, which brings a connection, something I'm remembering, which leads me to something else I'm remembering, which led me to another question I had about the text. When we're reading texts closely and accurately, that's what we're doing: We're thinking about our thinking, and we're thinking about what the author was really trying to say with the words that are on the page.

Now it's your turn to try it. As I read a line, you and your partner are going to turn and talk. Listen with a wide-awake mind. Attend to all the details

FIGURE 10.1. Mr. R.'s two-column chart for close reading.

closely and accurately. Then, talk using these same sentence starters I have used here [see Figure 10.2 for thought starters]. Let's have a go.

[Students try it for a few lines, talking after each line. Partners alternate turns talking. Students closely read their independent texts while Mr. R. confers with individual students.]

MR. R.: Let's think a little bit about what we were doing today. We were working on reading our texts closely, so that those details led us to have thoughts about what we were reading. And when we're doing that, we start to really understand what it is the author of that text was trying to say to us. How did reading in this way help you understand this book better? What types of things were you noticing? Lisa, go ahead.

LISA: It made you notice the details better because you were reading closely, and you were paying more attention to the text, instead of maybe speeding up and reading a little faster.

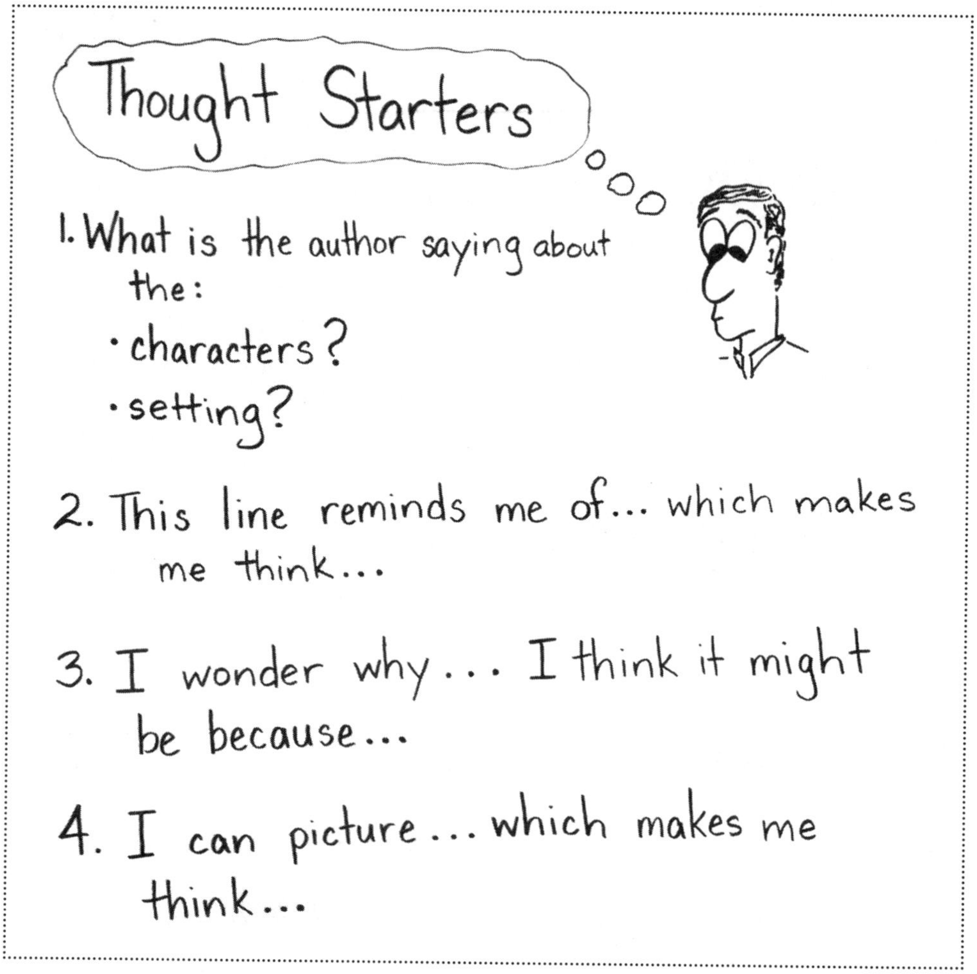

FIGURE 10.2. Mr. R.'s thought starters.

MR. R.: Yeah, instead of just reading past those words, you really had to focus. Other thoughts?

MARIA: I saw things I never thought I would have seen.

ELIZA: I had a question about who a character was, and it, like, quickly later on in the story said who it was, but if I wasn't reading slowly, I might have continued to have the question later on.

MR. R.: Anyone else have something to add?

DILLON: It made me understand the characters more, like, their personality. Like, the first time I read *The Jacket*, I read it quickly and didn't even know that one of the boys was white and the other one was black. So, this helped me understand it more.

MR. R.: And you were able to get deeper into that relationship. Molly?

MOLLY: I started to notice patterns that help to understand the characters, like, little patterns, even if they aren't big.

MR. R.: Can you say more about that?

MOLLY: Like, if they . . . something that they're always seeing or, like, when they pass, like, when they go to school, they always see something and they keep mentioning it, and then that later becomes important, but you wouldn't have noticed it if you weren't reading slow enough.

MR. R.: Noticing the small details sometimes brings you to something that's going to happen later, so it's almost like the author was putting it there for a reason, for what's going to come up, but when you read quickly you don't notice it.

WILL: It really slows down the book, and then with all the small details, they all tie into the big master plot of the book.

MR. R.: And as I said, it really slows down, but we don't read like this all of the time. Sometimes we really need to slow down on a book because it's especially complex or difficult and we are really trying to get what the author is trying to say.

ANGELA: Well, before, when I read the book, I thought it was dull and it didn't have any exciting features. But then when I put it on the two-column chart, it builds up more suspense, and now I know what the climax is, and . . . and now it's more exciting, and that's how I love to read books now.

MR. R.: Yeah, and I love how you brought it back to the story structure, too, because we worked on following that narrative story structure, but we want to connect our thoughts to that narrative story structure. So, readers, there's been some real growth today in the work that you're doing as thinking readers, and I don't want it to just be an isolated thing. This is the type of thinking that we want to be doing every day. When we read our texts in this way, we're going to really understand what the author was trying to say to us.

Your Turn: Talking the Talk!

1 Select a group of students that needs help reading texts closely.

2 Use the lesson template (Appendix A) to plan your lesson, thinking about the language choices you should make to help students understand and use close reading as a strategy to facilitate understanding.

- ◆ Talk the talk! Plan how you will connect this strategy to the students' reading goals. Pay special attention to how you will explain and model close reading.

- ◆ Plan how you will guide the students in practice. Select phrases, lines, and passages that exemplify meaningful places to apply the strategic action. As you guide students, emphasize *how* to use a range of strategic actions— literal and inferential—to understand the author's intended message.

- ◆ After teaching the lesson, reflect on the explicitness and clarity of your talk (Appendix B). How did it go? Did you use your talk to help students set goals, to explain and prompt students to read closely employing a range of strategic actions? Did you provide feedback that facilitated students' understanding of the text and close reading as a strategy? Appendix C provides three examples of teachers' responses to the reflection questions.

Lesson Plan 10: Close Reading

Common Core State Standard

◆ Literature Standard 1: Quote accurately from a text when explaining what the text says explicitly and when drawing inferences from the text.
◆ Literature Standard 2: Determine a theme of a story, drama, or poem from the details in the text, including how the characters in a story or drama respond to challenges or how the speaker in a poem reflects upon a topic; summarize the text.

Text

◆ *Fly Away Home*, by Eve Bunting

Set the Knowledge Goal

1 Understand how close reading helps us to deepen our understanding of ideas in a text.

2 Apply close reading to answer this question: When is a home more than the walls we live within?

Explain It

1 Explain that students will read texts closely to understand what the author was really trying the say.

2 Explain that close reading involves employing a range of strategic actions, literal and inferential, while thinking about the author's words in small chunks (e.g., one line, one paragraph).

3 Model how to read the text line by line, focusing students' attention on both the strategic actions being used as well as the text's evolving meaning.

Guide Practice

1 Prompt students to listen to the next two lines being read aloud. Have the students turn and talk about what those lines made them think.

- ◆ Prompting statements: "What just happened here? What does this make you think?"
- ◆ Elaborative statements: "Why are you thinking that?"

2 Prompt students to listen to the next two lines being read aloud. Again, have the students turn and talk.

3 Prompt students to share as a whole class what they were thinking and saying when turning to talk with their partners. The teacher provides facilitative feedback statements, such as the following:

- Feedback statements: "I noticed that _____ just made an inference about this line, which led him to make a connection to both his background knowledge and to prior knowledge gained from the text."

4 Prompt students to read their independent texts stopping every line or two. As they stop, have the students record their thinking on the two-column chart in Form 10.1 at the end of this chapter.

- What just happened?
- What does this make me think?

Recap and Reflect

- Remind students that reading closely requires them to pay extra attention to the author's ideas and consider them in relation to their own knowledge and experiences. Close reading will help them to deepen their understanding of the texts they are reading. Prompt them to share how the strategy was useful to them and to identify times when they might employ the strategy when reading.

Two-Column Chart for Close Reading

Name _____

Title _____   Author _____

What just happened?	What does this make me think?

Writing Instruction
Talking the Talk!

Writing is a complex and powerful act (Graham & Harris, 2011). A skill-ful writer is goal-driven, while also balancing the demands of both form (e.g., knowledge of letter sounds and symbols; knowledge of how to form letters and encode sounds heard; knowledge of sentence constructions and grammar; and knowledge of the characteristics of varied genres) and func-tion (e.g., purpose, audience) in writing (Graham & Harris, 2011). At the same time, a skillful writer is engaged in a social activity. Writing is shaped by the explicit and implicit relationship between the writer and reader and also by the larger cultural and social communities of which the writer and reader are a part (Graham & Harris, 2011; Roser & Bomer, 2005).

Writing serves varied functions for both the individual writer and the larger community. First, it is a powerful means of communication (Casbergue & Plauché, 2005; Roser & Bomer, 2005). Written correspon-dence now occurs in an array of forms, ranging from formal and informal letter writing and e-mail correspondence to instant messaging and texting. Although these forms of writing have clear differences, each shapes our social interactions in important ways. Second, writing conveys knowledge and ideas. Writers share their knowledge of the world and stories with read-ers through informational and narrative texts. Writers also sometimes write only for themselves—to develop and refine their own knowledge of topics of interest. In these ways writing is both a powerful means of self-reflection and also of self-expression (Dyson & Freedman, 1991; Graham & Harris, 2011). Writers deepen their understanding of their own identity through their intentions for writing, preferred types of writing, and interests in top-ics chosen.

Just as writing itself is a complex and multifaceted act, becoming a skillful and effective teacher of writing requires understanding and thoughtful orchestration of an equally complex base of knowledge. Skillful teachers of writing know how (1) to establish positive writing environments; (2) to provide explicit instruction of requisite writing skills and strategies; and (3) to develop rhetorical knowledge (e.g., genre, text structure) needed to communicate effectively and engage readers (Bromley, 2011; Calkins, 2003, 2006). Effective writing teachers operationalize these central ideas by implementing an array of specific actions, which may include:

- Maintaining high expectations for *all students* to write and write often.
- Engaging students in writing for real and important purposes that communicate and deepen learning.
- Ensuring that the writing done is valued by all in a risk-free environment.
- Fostering the identities of students as writers.
- Providing time, space, and the necessary materials for *all* students to be effective writers.
- Explicitly teaching and guiding students in *how* to engage in effective writing practices within varied genres and text types.

Within this positive learning environment, skillful writing teachers engage students in different approaches to writing, each with its own benefits to the writer. For example, students are taught to utilize a process approach (e.g., Calkins, 1994; Graves, 1983), engaging in planning, drafting, revising, editing, and publishing, and as they do so, they come to understand that effective writing evolves through a series of nonsequential "steps." Students are also taught about various forms and characteristics of literary genres (Donovan & Smolkin, 2006; Kamberelis, 1998) so that they come to understand how to select a text type to effectively communicate their message. Finally, teachers engage students in informal writing (e.g., brainstorming, free writing, journaling and response logs, graphic organizers) to acquire strategies to deepen and refine their own knowledge base and understanding of topics in preparation for writing (Graves et al., 2011).

In this section we provide examples of lessons that incorporate the type of teacher talk that helps students accomplish three important writing tasks: (1) planning to write an argument, (2) drafting a research report, and (3) writing to learn. We chose these particular tasks because of the close alignment with the CCSS in English language arts.

Planning to Write an Argument

What Is It?

Planning, or prewriting activities, are designed to help writers capture and organize their ideas. Informal writing such as brainstorming, journaling, and use of graphic organizers, as well as engaging in conversation with others, are all tools that writers can use to help them develop their thinking in relation to their chosen audience, purpose, and form.

Why Is It Important?

The CCSS in English language arts include an expectation that students will be able to write "logical arguments based on substantive claims, sound reasoning, and relevant evidence" (*www.corestandards.org/about-the-standards/key-points-in-english-language-arts*). Meeting this standard is unlikely without a thoughtful, focused plan that will guide both the collection of information to be shared and an organizational structure that will effectively convey the argument. Planning for writing is likely to support achievement of this standard because it

> provides external memory, where ideas can be stored without the risk of losing them and are readily available for inspection, reflection, and reconceptualization. Planning in advance can reduce the need to plan while writing, freeing needed resources to engage in other processes that demand attention, and turning ideas into well-crafted sentences. (Graham & Harris, 2007, p. 120)

Planning behavior is correlated with improved writing performance for writers of all abilities. However, studies indicate that many students do not approach writing with any sort of a written plan, and students with learning disabilities, in particular, do little planning even when prompted to do so (MacArthur & Graham, 1987). Students generally do not lack ideas for writing, but rather they have difficulty gaining access to those ideas as they write (Graham & Harris, 2011). When teachers explicitly engage students in prewriting strategies that guide them in accessing their store of knowledge, including ways to brainstorm words and ideas and generate and organize content, students improve both their use of planning strategies and the quality of their work (Graham & Harris, 2011; Graham & Perin, 2007).

When Do I Teach It?

Teach students planning strategies when you observe that their topics are not well-developed, and their writing lacks a clear organization.

What Do I Do?

Create an Instructional Context That Supports and Demands Planning.

As with almost all cognitive strategies, if we expect and anticipate that planning will become a routine part of our students' writing practices, we must help them to understand "why planning is important, how it helps the writer, and when to use it" (Graham & Harris, 2007, p. 123). To develop these understandings, Graham and Harris recommend that teachers:

- Establish predictable writing routines, engaging students in both individual and collaborative idea generation (e.g., brainstorming) and content organization before each writing assignment.
- Incorporate conversations about planning into writing conferences with discussion about how the writer intends to "get ready to write."
- Provide facilitative feedback on students' writing ideas, supporting and reinforcing productive ideas and redirecting and scaffolding further planning when necessary.

Set a Knowledge Goal.

Begin the lesson by reminding students of the knowledge goal they have been reading about and explain to them that they will use their newly acquired information to write an argument that will help their readers achieve the same knowledge goal.

Use Talk to Explain, Model, and Guide.

- Describe why students need to plan their writing to create clear and coherent compositions.

- Explain and show how to use a graphic organizer as a tool to support coherence and sufficient topic development.

- Guide students as they record their information within the sections of the graphic organizer.

- Notice and name (Johnston, 2004) the ways students use the organizer to effectively organize their writing, or, if they are not using it effectively, describe ways they might use it to more effectively organize their writing.

Recap and Reflect.

Discuss how the organizer breaks the planning process down into manageable chunks, while also making the characteristics of the particular genre explicit.

Example: Putting the Plan into Practice

In the following lesson excerpt, Ms. Nichols is working one-on-one with a sixth-grade writer, Carlos. Carlos had been reading and collecting information about the football player, Tim Tebow, from a variety of text sources (i.e., a biography and several websites) to consider whether Tebow could be considered a hero or not. With the guidance of Ms. Nichols, Carlos chose to write an argumentative essay defending his opinion of the football player. As you read the transcript, notice how Ms. Nichols first introduces the organizer in relation to writing an argument. (The student-completed organizer can be seen in Figure 11.1.) Then, notice how she supports Carlos with increasingly more explicit prompts and explanations as she guides him to complete the first part of the organizer. Finally, notice how Ms. Nichols reminds Carlos of the steps they completed together before he continues to fill in the organizer on his own.

Ms. N.: We have been focusing on research on Tim Tebow. What has your knowledge goal been?

Carlos: In what ways can Tim Tebow be considered a hero?

Ms. N.: All right. We talked a few days ago about what it means to be a hero, and we've recorded a few ideas about that here on this chart. And you've been thinking about those ideas as you've read these different pieces about Tim Tebow. Today we're going to focus on writing an argument and using this graphic organizer [Figure 11.1]. Since this is the first time that we're doing this type of writing, where you have to defend an opinion, I'm going to help you get started and then have you take over. We've used this particular graphic organizer before. Does it look familiar to you?

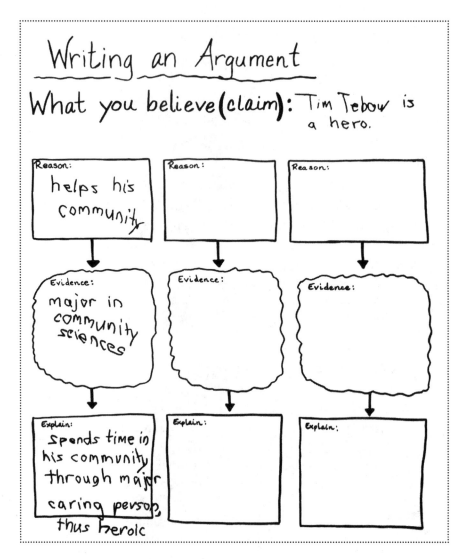

FIGURE 11.1. Student-created planning organizer for writing an argument.

CARLOS: Yeah.

MS. N.: Tell me a little bit about what you already know.

CARLOS: Well, basically you're kind of explaining. And when you're explaining, you're going back to the reasons. But then sometimes I think if you restate it, you have to restate it differently—like, make sure you put ideas in your own words. That's like a harder part.

MS. N.: Yeah, and I know we've talked about this before, but it's important to plan our ideas so that everything ties together. So while you're easily able to come up with the reasons as to why you believe something, and even evidence, you have to be able to explain all that to the audience in a way that's clear and organized to make people believe what you believe. Simply saying "because I said so" doesn't quite cut it. We have to add the reasons, the evidence, and the explanations to answer all of those "why" questions people will ask you about your opinion. Our focus question is: Do you consider Tim Tebow to be a hero? What do you think?

CARLOS: You mean, just jump right in?

MS. N.: Yes, but let's talk about it first because that will get you thinking about what you might want to write and help you start to organize your thinking.

CARLOS: So, let's see.

MS. N.: Let's get the notes that you have been collecting. Based on everything you now know and synthesizing the information, could I consider him a hero or a role model even?

CARLOS: OK. Well, he majored in community sciences, and that kind of makes me think he's caring.

MS. N.: That's true. Absolutely.

CARLOS: So, showing that he's caring in the evidence in community sciences, it would show that he's like helping his community and he's caring about what's around him.

MS. N.: OK.

CARLOS: And he takes it very seriously. Like his religion. He takes his religion very seriously.

MS. N.: How do you know that? Have you seen him do things, or did you read something about the way he follows his religion that convinces you that he takes his religion very seriously?

CARLOS: Yes. Like he kneels and prays before big plays and things like that. And I read that he goes to, like, hospitals and schools and orphanages and stuff and shares his faith. And I read that he's been doing the same things since he was in high school. It shows that he can stick to something and he's very persistent.

MS. N.: That's great. I love the word *persistent* as a descriptor for him. So, what I'm hearing with you throwing out these ideas here is that you, at the very start here (*pointing to the top of the organizer*), do you agree or disagree that he's a hero?

CARLOS: Ah, I think so.

MS. N.: You think he is. So let's at least start at that point: Tim Tebow is a hero.

CARLOS: (*Writes claim at the top of the organizer.*)

MS. N.: OK. Tim Tebow is a hero. Why?

CARLOS: He helps his community.

MS. N.: OK. He's community-oriented.

CARLOS: (*Writes in first Reason box.*) Helps his community.

MS. N.: How do you know? What evidence do you have?

CARLOS: Majored in community sciences. (*Writes in Evidence box.*)
(*reading organizer*) "Explain." He puts time into it?

MS. N.: Well, when you're doing the explaining part, you want to connect these two [Reason and Evidence]. So how does his major in community sciences show that he helps his community? And how does that ultimately make him a hero? So, it's kind of like two sentences: one connecting it to the reason, and one connecting it to the big idea.

CARLOS: OK, Tim Tebow's heroic caringness . . . no.

MS. N.: Well, that's not a word, but we're just talking this explanation through right now to help organize your thinking.

CARLOS: Tim Tebow's heroic kindness pays off in his community? With his college degree.

MS. N.: I think you're on the right track, but we need to think a little more about how we can organize this idea. To start, we're going to be really literal. I know when you do your writing, you like to add a lot of vocabulary and make it sound fancy, which is wonderful, but when we're starting . . .

CARLOS: Not for this.

MS. N.: Well, eventually for this, yeah. But when we're just starting, we're going to make it as simple as possible and then we'll grow from there.

CARLOS: OK.

MS. N.: So, his major is community science. How does that show that he's a hero, or that he cares about his community?

CARLOS: (*no response.*)

MS. N.: If you major in something, what does that mean?

CARLOS: Well, it's basically what you study a lot of in college.

MS. N.: Yes. Exactly. So by studying community sciences a lot, what does that show about him?

CARLOS: He puts a lot of time into his community.

MS. N.: There it is. That makes sense. Do you see how we connected these two ideas together and asked a question about it in order to explain?

CARLOS: That's what I was saying!

MS. N.: I know, but we made it a little more explicit.

CARLOS: (*Writes in Explanation box.*) He spends time devoted to his community through his major.

MS. N.: So, he spends a lot of time working in the community. Good. Or devoted to his community. Absolutely. By my major in education, it shows that I want to be a teacher and spend a lot of time doing that. By his major in community science, it shows that he wants to work with his community eventually. Good. So, how does spending time with your community show that you're a hero?

CARLOS: OK. So, like . . . so, he spends time in his community through his major, which is showing, although he's an athlete, he's still taking the time to study something that will help in his career in the future.

Ms. N.: True.

CARLOS: Which shows he's a good person.

Ms. N.: OK.

CARLOS: He's a good person, and uh . . .

Ms. N.: All of these are great thoughts. He's devoted to his major, which shows he's a good person. We can probably come up with a better word for *good* later.

CARLOS: He's a *caring* person.

Ms. N.: OK.

CARLOS: (*Writes in Explanation box.*) He's caring, and thus, heroic.

Ms. N.: So, what did we do there? In your own words, how would you break that [organizer] down?

CARLOS: I said my opinion, and then I thought of a reason why. Then I wrote evidence for my reason. And then I . . .

Ms. N.: Great so far. And then you explained the connection between your evidence and your reason, and between your evidence and your initial opinion. Great work. Let's continue with your next reason. I want you to try it out as much as possible on your own first, and then we'll discuss.

[The lesson continues with Carlos taking more responsibility for organizing thinking.]

Your Turn: Talking the Talk!

1 Select a group of students who need help planning their writing and developing coherent topics.

2 Use the lesson template (Appendix A) to plan your lesson thinking about the language choices you should make to help students understand and plan how to organize their writing effectively.

◆ Talk the talk! Plan how you will connect this strategy to the students' writing goals. Pay special attention to how you will explain and model planning.

◆ Plan how you will guide the students in practice. As you guide students, emphasize *how* to use graphic organizers to coherently develop a topic.

◆ After teaching the lesson, reflect on the explicitness and clarity of your talk (Appendix B). How did it go? Did you use your talk to help students set goals, to explain and prompt students to plan for well-developed topics? Did you provide feedback that facilitated students' understanding of planning as a strategy for more effective writing? Appendix C provides three examples of teachers' responses to the reflection questions.

Lesson Plan 11: Planning to Write an Argument

Common Core State Standard

◆ Writing Standard 1: Write arguments to support claims with clear reasons and relevant evidence.

Text

◆ *Through My Eyes*, by Tim Tebow and Nathan Whitaker
◆ *Tim Tebow Fans, www.timtebowfans.org/tim-tebow-biography.php*
◆ *Tim Tebow.biography, www.biography.com/people/tim-tebow-20786869*
◆ *Tim Tebow Foundation, www.timtebowfoundation.org*

Set the Knowledge Goal

1 To understand why planning is important to effective writing.

2 To use planning to prepare a strong and compelling argument about why (or why not) Tim Tebow should be considered a hero.

Explain

1 Explain that students will be writing an argument to support their opinion about Tim Tebow as a hero or not. Remind them that the notes they have been recording over the last several days may be helpful as they plan their response.

2 Discuss the meaning of *hero*. What characteristics, qualities, or achievements define *heroism?*

3 Explain that an effective argument provides a claim, while also providing reasons, evidence, and explanations to support the claim. The teacher provides a graphic organizer that has space for each of these important features of argument writing. A template for this organizer can be found in Form 11.1 at the end of this chapter.

Guide Practice

1 Prompt students to first discuss the information they collected related to the knowledge goal (Is Tim Tebow a hero? Why or why not?). Prompt students to make a claim based on the information they collected and to write the claim at the top of the organizer.

◆ Prompting statement: "Is Tim Tebow a hero?"

◆ Elaborative statements: "Why or why not? Can you say more about that?"

2 Prompt students to elaborate with additional evidence or examples to support their point of view.

- ◆ Elaborative statements: "Can you be more specific? Can you provide an example or an instance that supports your point of view?"

3 Prompt students to explain the connection between their evidence and their reason and between their evidence and their initial claim.

- ◆ Clarifying statements: "I think you need to be more explicit here. I don't quite see how your evidence supports your initial claim."

4 Prompt students to follow the same procedures as they continue to fill in the rest of the graphic organizer. Guide students' work with statements such as those previously described.

Recap and Reflect

- ◆ Remind students of the importance of effective planning in developing well-written pieces. Discuss the step-by-step planning procedures students need to use to prepare to write with clarity and coherence.

Writing an Argument

Name _____

What you believe (claim):

Reason:	**Reason:**	**Reason:**

↓ ↓ ↓

Evidence:	**Evidence:**	**Evidence:**

↓ ↓ ↓

Explain:	**Explain:**	**Explain:**

Drafting a Research Report

What Is It?

Drafting is the process of transcribing thoughts into print. There are different approaches to drafting. In one approach, emphasis is placed on idea generation and formation with little attention to "polishing" ideas. Proponents of this approach argue that without attention to carefully crafting the ideas, writers are free to devote all of their cognitive attention to idea generation. As a result, their final texts—those that come with revision—contain a greater number of ideas (Glynn, Britton, Muth, & Dogun, 1982).

Others argue, however, that writing is a more iterative and recursive process such that the very act of composing prompts the writer to think of additional and often very different ideas. In this view, these ideas do not result from sequential steps of first drafting and then revising, but rather emerge during a process in which drafting and revising occur in interaction with each other, prompting writers to think about ideas in new ways and leading to the discovery of new knowledge (Elbow, 1973).

These somewhat conflicting ideas have reminded us of the importance of taking an instructional stance that allows more than one pathway to learning and achievement. It is likely that in our classrooms we will have writers who take different approaches, and we must allow freedom for them to do so. This requires careful "kidwatching" (Goodman, 1978)—that is, observing our students during the drafting process and noticing precisely what they do, and then allowing them the freedom to pursue the process in a way that is most productive for them. This does not mean that "anything goes" but rather that we acknowledge that different students enact planning, drafting, and revising in different ways. We must keep our focus on the purpose of the process as a whole—to guide students to compose a coherent and engaging text that advances knowledge (either that of the writer or the reader, or, in the best circumstance, both!). To lead us toward the realization of that purpose, we must combine our knowledge of research and our awareness and understanding of the students in our classroom in ways that optimize their opportunities to learn.

Why Is It Important?

The fundamental notion behind drafting as an important step in the writing process is that the first transcription of our ideas into print represents a type of rehearsal or work in progress, and that repeatedly engaging in all of the stages of the writing process (planning, drafting, revising, editing) leads the writer to discover meaning that might otherwise remain hidden. In turn, then, when writers are taught explicit strategies for engaging in each step of the writing process, and given time to exercise each of the processes, the quality of their work improves (Graham & Perin, 2007).

When Do I Teach It?

Even though students have captured and organized their thoughts in some form of a plan for writing, they still struggle when trying to get their ideas down on paper.

What Do I Do?

Create a Classroom Context That Supports All Stages of the Writing Process.

Writing experts tell us that *becoming* a writer (as opposed to learning how to write) requires immersing our students within an instructional context in which they receive explicit instruction in research-based writing strategies and in which they are provided sufficient time for the routines in which "real" writers engage (e.g., Graham & Harris, 2007; Graham & Perin, 2007). For example, although at times we all write quickly and on demand, much published writing is composed over time. Accomplished writers ponder a number of possibilities for writing topics and the point of view or stance they will take on a topic or an issue; they gather information and build background knowledge, they draft and revise and share their thoughts—in the early stages, along the way, and/or in the later stages—and eventually they prepare a final piece and publish it for others to read. These writing behaviors and activities require time and practice, and they also demand routinization. That is, accomplished writers establish a writing routine—they have expectations for when and where they will write. Developing writers, too, need to know that these behaviors and activities will be part of their classroom community—that they can count on excellent instruction *and* a consistent time and place when they can enact the behaviors and activities that are characteristic of "real" writers. Developing writers also need to know that with opportunity comes accountability—that is, they will be expected to exercise these behaviors and participate in the activities.

Set a Knowledge Goal.

Begin the lesson by explaining to students that they will use the notes they had previously taken to help them answer their research questions and to prepare a draft of their research report.

Use Talk to Explain, Model, and Guide.

- Explain and show how to use notes to compose a rough draft of their ideas. Emphasize that students will have time to return to their draft to revise and polish it, to add or delete information, improve the organizational coherence, or make different language choices to more effectively capture their ideas.
- Guide students as they make decisions about how to organize and present their ideas. Maintain the focus on the students as the authors of the writing and encourage them to read their writing aloud.
- Notice and name (Johnston, 2004) students' particular word choices, sentence constructions, and organization and how they support (or could be improved to better support) the ideas that they are trying to convey.

Recap and Reflect.

Remind students of the process they used to draft their research reports, highlighting the types of questions and considerations writers make that lead to coherent and engaging writing.

Example: Putting the Plan into Practice

In the following lesson excerpt, Ms. Bates continues her work on researching tigers with her second-grade group. The students had finished their shared research and were now ready to start drafting their research reports. As you read the transcript, notice how Ms. Bates first explains how they are going to approach the writing, and then she guides them line by line as to how they might use their notes to write a coherent paragraph. At times, Ms. Bates seems to be engaging students in an ongoing process of drafting and revision—they don't simply put their first thoughts down on the page. In this example, they collaboratively discuss ideas and ways to craft their ideas. We suspect that Ms. Bates has found that in this group of emerging writers, this process of guided, collaborative writing is a necessary step as these youngsters develop strategies for independent writing. In addition, notice that even as she offers guidance and suggestions when drafting, she reminds the students that they are the authors of their pieces and that they must make the final decision. By doing so, she is able to establish the students' identities as writers and foster their motivation to continue this work on their own after the group session.

MS. B.: Today we're going to start to draft the ideas we have been collecting about tigers. We talked earlier about how we wanted our writing to be in a question-and-answer format like we had seen in some of the informational books we were browsing through. So our headings for each section will be one of the questions you all generated when we started our research, and then we will use the notes that we collected as we read *Endangered Tigers* to draft each section of the report. We'll draft the first one together, and then I'm going to have each of you try to continue on your own. What question should we start with today?

VINCENT: What do tigers eat?

MS. B.: OK, let's write that down at the top of our papers. What do tigers eat?

ALL: (*writing*)

MS. B.: Okay, now how do you think we should start? Should we just write down "Deer, elk, wild pig, birds, cows, monkey, lizards," just like that? Will that make sense to our readers?

LUIS: No!

MS. B.: I don't think so either, Luis. We need to add a little bit more than that. How could we start it, though?

LUIS: Tigers are predators.

MS. B.: Ohhhhh, I like it. I like how you are incorporating that vocabulary word that we have been using. It tells the reader something important about tigers. Let's write it down.

ALL: (*writing*)

VINCENT: (*subvocalizing while writing*) Tigers . . . are . . . pre . . . (*spelling*) P, R, E, D, A, T, O, R, S.

MS. B.: Vincent, I like how you referenced your notes when you weren't sure how to write *predator*. That was smart thinking, don't you think so, Raphael?

RAPHAEL: Yeah, I did that, too.

MS. B.: Great. So, let's look at *predator* on our word board. Our meaning for predator was what?

LUIS: (*reading*) "Predators are animals that hunt and eat other animals."

MS. B.: So, let's see now. Predators hunt and eat other animals. How could we use that definition to help us in our writing. We want to try to use all of these great tiger words as much as possible to make our writing more specific. What could we say about tigers now?

VINCENT: We could say, "Tigers are predators because they eat pigs, cows, birds, lizards, and crocodiles."

MS. B.: OK. That gives us more information about how tigers are predators, but should we make that all part of the same sentence? Tigers are predators because they eat all of these things.

RAPHAEL: We can make a new sentence. "Tigers are predators." Then . . .

MS. B.: Good. Two sentences will work better. What could our second sentence be, using the great ideas Vincent gave us from the definition?

VINCENT: We can write, "They are predators because they hunt and eat other animals."

MS. B.: Oh, so now we have two sentences. "Tigers are predators. They are predators because they hunt and eat other animals." What do you think? Does that make sense?

LUIS: Yeah.

RAPHAEL: I think so.

MS. B.: I think you're right. It works. We might even decide not to say *predators* twice. We could write, "Tigers are predators. They hunt and eat other animals." That would work, too, but you guys need to decide because you are the authors here. How should we say it?

VINCENT: I think it should be "They hunt and eat other animals."

LUIS: Me too.

MS. B.: OK, let's write that. This second sentence gives the reason why they are predators in case our reader doesn't know what a *predator* is.

ALL: (*writing*)

MS. B.: All right, let's reread our writing so far to see if it makes sense.

ALL: (*reading*) "Tigers are predators. They hunt and eat other animals."

MS. B.: Now, what do we need to say next? What should we tell our reader next?

LUIS: They . . . they eat . . . birds.

MS. B.: We can write, "They eat birds." Maybe later we can think of another one of our great tiger words to use in this sentence.

RAPHAEL: *Prey!*

VINCENT: Yeah! They eat their prey!

MS. B.: Oh, so our next sentence could be, "They eat their prey." Should we write that for now?

LUIS: Yeah.

ALL: (*writing*)

RAPHAEL: Wait, is it *T, H, E, I, R?*

MS. B.: Yes, that is correct way to write that word in this sentence. Now what do we need to make sure we include?

RAPHAEL: What they eat?

MS. B.: Right? How should we write that?

VINCENT: "They eat birds, pigs, lizards, and cows."

MS. B.: OK, so now we can use our notes to list the types of animals that tigers hunt and eat. Can each of you now use the notes to write your next sentence?

ALL: (*writing*)

MS. B.: Great! So we wrote this section together. We put the question at the top as our heading, and then we wrote sentences that first described tigers as predators. Then we used our notes to add in specific details about the kinds of animals that tigers eat. What should our next section be?

LUIS: Where do tigers live?

RAPHAEL: Yeah.

MS. B.: All right, I want you guys to go back to your desks and use our model here to begin writing this next section: "Where do tigers live?" Tomorrow we'll share our thinking about this section to see how we can help each other revise.

Your Turn: Talking the Talk!

1 Select a group of students that needs help drafting their thoughts in an organized manner.

2 Use the lesson template (Appendix A) to plan your lesson, thinking about the language choices you should make to help students understand how to transfer notes from an organizer to a drafted piece of writing.

   ◆ Talk the talk! Plan how you will connect this work to the students' writing goals. Pay special attention to how you will explain and model the drafting process.

   ◆ Plan how you will guide the students in practice. As you guide students, encourage them to refer to their written notes to support writing fluency and accuracy.

   ◆ After teaching the lesson, reflect on the explicitness and clarity of your talk (Appendix B). How did it go? Did you use your talk to help students set goals, to explain and prompt students to draft effectively? Did you provide feedback that facilitated students' understanding of why certain choices make more sense than others when writing pieces that are clearly organized and well developed? Appendix C provides three examples of teachers' responses to the reflection questions.

Lesson Plan 12: Drafting A Research Report

Common Core State Standard

◆ Writing Standard 2: Write informative/explanatory texts in which they introduce a topic, use facts and definitions to develop points, and provide a concluding statement or section.

◆ Writing Standard 7: Participate in shared research and writing projects (e.g., read a number of books on a single topic to produce a report; record science observations).

Text

◆ *Endangered Tigers*, by Bobbie Kalman

Set the Knowledge Goal

1. What are the physical characteristics of tigers?

2 How have tigers adapted to living in their environments?

Explain

1 Explain that students will be drafting their research reports using the notes they organized while reading for information. Guide the students to choose an appropriate format for the informational writing based on browsing through a variety of texts to notice organizational features.

2 Explain how students need to think and talk about how they might compose their sentences to ensure clarity and organization.

Guide Practice

1 Prompt students to consider how they might start their writing. Ensure that the students have provided a topic sentence or main idea sentence that can then be developed further with details.

- ◆ Prompting statements: "How should we start? What should we include at the beginning of our section?"

- ◆ Clarifying statements: "Should we combine these two ideas together into one sentence, or leave them as two separate sentences? Do you think that sentence gives away too many details too early in the piece? Does that sound like the information in books we have read?"

2 Prompt students to consider how their paragraph will develop as they provide more specific details to their support their topic sentence.

- ◆ Elaborative statement: "Can we provide more specific information here to say more about this idea?"

- ◆ Feedback statement: "I like how you are using some of our words from our word board to provide a more descriptive answer to the question."

Recap and Reflect

◆ Remind students that they are drafting an answer to their question headings. In doing so, discuss how they first chose a question, then wrote a general statement as an answer, and finally, used their notes to support their statement with specific details. Discuss how rereading their own writing aloud helps writers develop clear sentences that are organized in a coherent manner.

Writing to Learn

What Is It?

Writing is often used as a tool to help people learn, think about, and understand new information. Graves et al. (2011) explain that, "In this kind of writing, students are actually 'thinking on paper' or perhaps on a computer screen" (p. 382). Writing to learn can take many forms, such as note taking, brainstorming, journaling and reading logs, or using various graphic organizers, and the form chosen depends on the purpose one brings to the task.

Why Is It Important?

Writing to learn in its various forms helps students to clarify, refine, and reflect on meaning when they are reading or viewing texts (Elbow, 1973; Graham & Harris, 2011). This more informal type of writing generally does not go through the various stages of the writing process (i.e., planning, drafting, revising, editing); rather, it is a spontaneous form of writing that provides a way to convey, preserve, and transmit knowledge (Graves et al., 2011; Roser & Bomer, 2005).

When Do I Teach It?

Provide instruction in strategies for writing to learn when you observe that, when students write in response to reading, they are unable to organize their thinking in coherent or systematic ways.

What Do I Do?

Select Meaningful Purpose for Writing in Response to Reading.

We noted that writing in response to reading, or writing to learn, is an important strategy for helping readers to clarify and remember information. One of our challenges as teachers is to think carefully about when and why we prompt students to write in response to reading. How will the writing-to-learn task advance students toward the knowledge goal? When and how will students use the information they record? For example, why might we ask them to take notes about a character's traits, actions, motives? Will they use these notes to compose a description of the character or to examine character changes over the course of a novel? Alternatively, will they take detailed notes about a character so that they can study an author's craft and examine the ways the author used language or other writing "props" to help the character come alive? As you prepare for a lesson on writing to learn, stay focused on the fundamental purpose of the lesson—writing in response to reading must be in the service of an important knowledge goal. How will students use their notes to deepen their understanding about an important idea?

Set a Knowledge Goal.

Begin the lesson by connecting a specific writing-to-learn task (e.g., note taking) to the writer's purpose of gathering new information to answer specified questions.

Use Talk to Explain, Model, and Guide.

- Describe why students should organize their thinking in ways that will support recall and understanding of the new information.
- Explain and show that the ways writers organize information depends on the purpose.
- Guide students as they organize information.
- Notice and name (Johnston, 2004) the organizational strategies the students are using and describe how the strategies support (or could be improved to support) their learning goals.

Recap and Reflect.

Discuss how writing to learn helps students to clarify and recall what they read.

Example: Putting the Plan into Practice

In the following lesson excerpt, Ms. Lynne is conferring with a fourth-grade writer, Chanelle, as she is writing to learn information about animals in China. In the context of the writing workshop that Ms. Lynne has established, Chanelle knows that she can use writing to learn as a way to also support other forms of writing. They have been analyzing various versions of the Little Red Riding Hood tale when reading, and Chanelle has decided that she would like to write her own version and have the story take place in China. As you read the transcript, notice how Ms. Lynne first engages Chanelle in a discussion of how her writing work is going so far to get a sense of her knowledge of writing to learn. Ms. Lynne then provides specific feedback validating the work that Chanelle is taking on as a writer and provides a model of how she might make this work more effective and efficient.

Ms. L.: How's it going?

CHANELLE: Good. I'm taking notes on all the animals that live in China because I want to write my own version of Little Red Riding Hood and have it be in China. Many kinds of animals live in China—tigers, monkeys, leopards, pandas, elephants, birds.

Ms. L.: That's great! It is so smart to collect information about a setting when you are planning to write a story. That way, the setting rings true to the reader because you are able to describe it and choose characters that will match what people know about the place. You know what? Some of these animals live in the forest, some live in the jungles, and some live in the deserts. It might help you to organize your notes around the different places where these animals live. Then, you can go back and add specific information about the environment and what it's like in each place. Can I show you?

CHANELLE: Yeah.

Ms. L.: Here. What's our main heading? What should that be?

CHANELLE: Animals.

Ms. L.: Animals. (*Writes heading on paper.*) Now, when I'm taking notes, instead of having just a big list of the animals, we could organize them into categories. That will help us to learn and remember the information because our brains like to think in patterns or groups. It helps us make sense of all of the information we are learning. So it says . . .

CHANELLE: (*reading*) "Tigers and leopards live in China's northern forest."

Ms. L.: So I'm going to write over here *Northern Forest*. And what should I write under this subheading?

CHANELLE: The animals that live there.

Ms. L.: Right. So what animals live in the northern forest?

CHANELLE: Tigers. Pandas. Do pandas live over there?

Ms. L.: How can you check?

CHANELLE: (*scanning text*) I guess not in the northern forest, but maybe somewhere else.

Ms. L.: Good. So you were able to check your understanding by going back to the text to confirm a question that you had.

CHANELLE: Tigers and leopards.

MS. L.: OK. (*writing*) Do you see how I listed only the animals that belonged in this category? Organizing our notes like this will help us remember this information and find it more easily if we need to revisit our notes and write more about it. Now you go ahead. What could the next category be?

CHANELLE: Jungle. (*Writes heading.*) Camels. (*writing*) Camels? That's weird.

MS. L.: I like how you're noticing that. What could you do to help you clarify?

CHANELLE: Reread.

MS. L.: Great strategy.

CHANELLE: (*scanning through the text*)

MS. L.: Are the camels in the jungle?

CHANELLE: Nope.

MS. L.: Good catch. I like how you questioned yourself about information that didn't make sense and then reread to confirm. That was a smart strategy to use. So, now that you've reread, who's in the jungle?

CHANELLE: Monkeys!

MS. L.: Monkeys and . . .

CHANELLE: Elephants. (*Writing*).

MS. L.: OK. Do you see how you are organizing your notes right now in a way that categorizes them into groups? How are those groups categorized?

CHANELLE: By the places where the animals are.

MS. L.: Right. You're grouping the information that we are learning about animals in China into the areas where those animals are found. Then you'll be able to revisit these notes and add more information about the animals' habitats, the food they eat, and other information you think might be important. Do you understand what we have been doing here?

CHANELLE: Yes.

MS. L.: So, what are you going to do now as you continue on your own?

CHANELLE: I'm going to write my next place, and then I'm going to read through the text to see what animals live in that area.

MS. L.: Right. You write your subheading, and then you write the details that go under that subheading. Good. How's this going to help you continue?

CHANELLE: I'll be able to find the information quicker when I need to remember which animals live in a certain place.

MS. L.: Great. It's going to help you learn and remember all of this new information more easily, and therefore, help you when you develop the setting and characters for you story. I'm going to check back with you tomorrow to see how this is going.

Your Turn: Talking the Talk!

1 Select a group of students that needs help writing to learn.

2 Use the lesson template (Appendix A) to plan your lesson, thinking about the language choices you should make to help students understand and use a strategy (e.g., note taking, semantic mapping, Venn diagram) to organize information learned for more efficient retrieval.

◆ Talk the talk! Plan how you will connect this strategy work to the students' reading and writing goals. Pay special attention to how you will explain and model writing to learn.

◆ Plan how you will guide the students in practice. As you guide students, emphasize *how* to use writing to learn as a way to understand and remember new information.

◆ After teaching the lesson, reflect on the explicitness and clarity of your talk (Appendix B). How did it go? Did you use your talk to help students set goals, to explain and prompt students to write as a way to facilitate learning new information? Did you provide feedback that supported students' understanding of writing to learn as a strategy? Appendix C provides three examples of teachers' responses to the reflection questions.

Lesson Plan 13: Writing to Learn

Common Core State Standard

◆ Writing Standard 8: Recall relevant information from experiences or gather relevant information from print and digital sources; take notes, categorize information, and provide a list of sources.

◆ Writing Standard 10: Write routinely over extended time frames (time for research, reflection, and revision) and shorter time frames (a single sitting or a day or two) for a range of discipline-specific tasks, purposes, and audiences.

Texts

◆ *China*, by Hugh Sebag-Montefiore
◆ *Welcome to China*, by Caryn Jenner
◆ *Kidepede: Chinese Animals*, www.historyforkids.org/learn/china/environment/animals.htm
◆ *Animals of China*, www.tooter4kids.com/china/animals_of_china.htm

Set the Knowledge Goal

◆ Organizing our note taking helps us to learn and remember information. What animals live in China?

Explain

1 Explain that writers organize their notes into categories so that information can more easily be remembered and retrieved when needed. The teacher explains that building associations between types of information helps us to remember.

2 Model how to set up note taking in a way that facilitates categorical thinking. Use a heading, subheadings, and details format.

Guide Practice

1 Prompt students to notice how the information from the texts is being organized as you model the first category.

  ◆ Prompting statement: "Do you see how I am putting these details together because they are part of the same group?"

  ◆ Clarifying statements: "Does that animal belong in this group? How can you check your understanding?"

2 Prompt students to determine the next category's subheading and then read to determine what information should be included. The teacher scaffolds students' work with specific feedback.

  ◆ Feedback statement: "I like how you are rereading the text as a way to confirm your information."

Recap and Reflect

◆ Discuss with the students the process used to organize new information into categories. Prompt the students to share how this work is helping them further develop their writing.

Lesson Template

Lesson Plan: _____   Student(s): _____

Common Core State Standard

Text

Set the Knowledge Goal(s)

Explain

Guide Practice

Recap and Respond

Reflecting on Your Own Talk

As you think about the lesson you just taught, reflect on the qualities of your instructional talk using the following questions as a guide.

1 What are your impressions of your talk?

 ◆ Goal-setting talk: How did you use your talk to help students set meaningful knowledge goals for themselves as learners?

 ◆ Explanatory talk: How did you use your talk to explain and prompt students to engage in strategic thinking?

 ◆ Feedback talk: How did you use your talk to provide feedback that explicitly facilitates students' understanding of content and also their understanding of reading and writing processes?

Some Examples of Reflecting on Your Own Talk

EXAMPLE 1

Lesson 1: Directly Teaching Word Meanings

Teacher: Ms. Needham

Students: Adam, Greg, Sarah

As you think about the lesson you just taught, reflect on the qualities of your instructional talk using the following questions as a guide.

1 What are your impressions of your talk?

◆ Goal-setting talk: How did you use your talk to help students set meaningful knowledge goals for themselves as learners?

I like how I asked the students to check the anchor chart we had created. I always think it is important for them to understand the purpose of those charts around the room. And then I remembered to have them think about authority in more of a real-world setting, so I think that went well too.

◆ Explanatory talk: How did you use your talk to explain and prompt students to engage in strategic thinking?

I thought I explained the definition of authority OK at the beginning when I referred them to the chart and then gave the police officer example. At the end, I did explain how knowing the word authority was helping their understanding of characters in Holes. I kind of used that to set a purpose for further reading, but I think I could have been more explicit there. Maybe ask them specifically to think about if Stanley's authority changes since he was the main character.

◆ Feedback talk: How did you use your talk to provide feedback that explicitly facilitates students' understanding content, and also their understanding of reading and writing processes?

With feedback, I think I was prompting the students to think more about the responses—like when I asked Adam if he agreed with Greg's response. I also kind of rephrased some of their thinking that I thought was good to kind of emphasize that point. I'm not sure if that came across to the students as I had intended, though. I might need to be more focused in those places.

(continued)

EXAMPLE 2

Lesson 2: Inferring Word Meaning through Context

Teacher: Ms. Wells

Student: Ana

As you think about the lesson you just taught, reflect on the qualities of your instructional talk using the following questions as a guide.

1. What are your impressions of your talk?

   ◆ Goal-setting talk: How did you use your talk to help students set meaningful knowledge goals for themselves as learners?

   I was so focused on making sure that Ana was using context clues that I never stated our goal again at the beginning. I remembered this at the end of the lesson and had a brief discussion about it, but it would have been better to be reading for that goal all along.

   ◆ Explanatory talk: How did you use your talk to explain and prompt students to engage in strategic thinking?

   I did prompt Ana several times to use the context to figure out the unfamiliar words. I like how I did prompt her to go back into the text a few different times and how we revisited the meaning of the words after the fact to help her with her comprehension. I did mention rereading and finding clues, but I think I could have done a much better job with a brief explanation of what context clues were. Even though we had done this before, Ana seemed a little unsure about what good clues would be.

   ◆ Feedback talk: How did you use your talk to provide feedback that explicitly facilitates students' understanding content, and also their understanding of reading and writing processes?

   I like when I gave the definition back to Ana and provided an elaboration on the meaning. I also made sure that I acknowledged her responses but refocused her when the clues were not really on. I also like that I tied the meaning of the words to our work on character traits, but I don't think I really linked the work between context clues and character traits very clearly.

   (continued)

EXAMPLE 3

Lesson 4: Visualizing

Teacher: Mr. Peterson

Students: Ariv, Kelly, Dominic, Jack

As you think about the lesson you just taught, reflect on the qualities of your instructional talk using the following questions as a guide.

1. What are your impressions of your talk?

   ◆ Goal-setting talk: How did you use your talk to help students set meaningful knowledge goals for themselves as learners?

   I need to try to be more concise at the beginning and keep the pace a little quicker. I did start right out by reminding the kids that we were trying to figure out how our actions affect other people. I liked that I gave them the goal as a reminder out front, but I took too long to get to the visualizing practice.

   ◆ Explanatory talk: How did you use your talk to explain and prompt students to engage in strategic thinking?

   I noticed at the beginning that I sort of explained that it was a good idea to go back and recap or summarize what had happened. And I said it was a good idea, but I don't think I said enough about why it was a good idea. For visualizing, I wanted them to get the what you do, when you do it, why you do it, how you do it, but I think my talk needs to be a little more explicit. I needed to say more and maybe provide an example or model.

   ◆ Feedback talk: How did you use your talk to provide feedback that explicitly facilitates students' understanding content, and also their understanding of reading and writing processes?

   I responded "good" to one kid, but it wasn't specific. And then another time, I did specifically say that a kid made an inference, but then I never defined it for the other kids. We had talked about inferences, but it could help these particular students to define it again. I did specifically provide feedback to one student who went back into the text for evidence. Overall, I need to be more explicit.

Children's Literature That Supports Visualization

Aliki. (1998). *Painted words and spoken memories*. New York: Greenwillow Books.

Baylor, B. (1995). *I'm in charge of celebrations*. New York: Aladdin.

Brinckloe, J. (1986). *Fireflies*. New York: Aladdin.

Coles, R. (1995). *The story of ruby bridges*. New York: Scholastic Press. (Common Core State Standards Book List)

Cooney, B. (1985). *Miss Rumphius*. New York: Puffin. (National Book Award)

Cowley, J. 1998). *Big moon tortilla*. Honesdale, PA: Boyds Mills Press.

Dorros, A. (1997). *Abuela*. New York: Puffin.

Fletcher, R. (2003). *Harvest moon*. New York: Clarion Books.

George, E. L. (2004). *Weaving the rainbow*. New York: Atheneum.

Grimes, N. (2001). *A pocketful of poems*. New York: Clarion Books.

Hooper, M. (2000). *River story*. Cambridge, MA: Candlewick Press.

MacLachlan, P. (1985). *Sarah, plain and tall*. New York: Harper Trophy. (Common Core State Standards Book List; Newbery Award)

Mazer, A. (1994). *The salamander room*. New York: Dragonfly Books.

McCloskey, R. (1989). *Time of wonder*. New York: Puffin. (Caldecott Award)

McLerran, A. (2004). *Roxaboxen*. New York: HarperCollins.

Rylant, C. (1991). *Night in the country*. New York: Atheneum Books.

Steig, W. (1986). *Brave Irene*. New York: Farrar, Straus, Giroux.

Stewart, M. (2009). *Under the snow*. Atlanta, GA: Peachtree.

Stewart, S. (2007). *The gardener*. New York: Farrar, Straus, Giroux.

Stringer, L. (2001). *Castles, caves, and honeycombs*. Orlando, FL: Harcourt.

Stringer, L. (2006). *Winter is the warmest season*. Orlando, FL: Harcourt.

Winter, J. (2007). *Angelina's Island*. New York: Farrar, Straus, Giroux.

White, E. B. (1952). *Charlotte's web*. New York: HarperCollins. (Common Core State Standards Book List; Newbery Award Honor)

Children's Literature That Supports Making Inferences

Agee, J. (2005). *Terrific*. New York: Hyperion.

Baylor, B. (1986). *Hawk, I'm your brother*. New York: Aladdin.

Brown, M. (1947). *Stone soup*. New York: Charles Scribner's Sons.

Curtis, C. P. (2007). *Elijah of buxton*. New York: Scholastic Press. (Coretta Scott King Award; Newbery Award Honor)

dePaola, T. (1982). *Charlie needs a cloak*. New York: Aladdin.

Fleischman, P. (2002). *Weslandia*. New York: Candlewick.

Fletcher, R. (1997). *Twilight comes twice*. New York: Clarion Books.

Garland, S. (1997). *Lotus Seed*. Orlando, FL: Harcourt.

Henkes, K. (2004). *Kitten's first full moon*. New York: Greenwillow Books. (Common Core State Standards Book List; Caldecott Award)

Kimmel, E. (2009). *The three little tamales*. Tarrytown, New York: Marshall Cavendish.

Kitamura, S. (1999). *Me and my cat?* New York: Farrar, Straus, Giroux.

Kitamura, S. (2005). *Pablo the artist*. New York: Farrar, Straus, Giroux.

LaMarche, J. (2002). *The raft*. New York: HarperCollins.

Lester, H. (1988). *Tacky the penguin*. Boston: Houghton Mifflin.

Levine, H. (2007). *Henry's freedom box: A true story from the underground railroad*. New York: Scholastic.

Lin, G. (2008). *Where the mountain meets the moon*. (Common Core State Standards Book List; Newbery Medal)

Newman, M. (2002). *Mole and the baby bird*. New York: Bloomsbury Children's Books.

Park, L. S. (2001). *A single shard*. New York: Sandpiper. (Newbery Award)

Paterson, K. (1978). *The great gilly hopkins*. New York: Harper Trophy. (National Book Award; Newbery Award Honor)

Polacco, P. (1998). *The bee tree*. New York: Puffin.

Sendak, M. (1963). *Where the wild things are*. New York: HarperCollins. (Caldecott Award)

Shannon G. (2007). *Rabbit's gift*. Orlando, FL: Harcourt.

Stevens, J. (1995). *Tops and bottoms*. Orlando, FL: Harcourt. (Common Core State Standards Book List, Caldecott Award Honor, IRA-CBC Children's Choice)

Tsuchiya, Y. (1997). *Faithful elephants: A true story of animals, people, and war*. Boston: Houghton Mifflin.

Van Allsburg, C. (1983). *Wreck of the Zephyr*. Boston: Houghton Mifflin.

Weisner, D. (1991). *Tuesday*. New York: Clarion Books. (Caldecott Award)

Woodson, J. (2001). *The other side*. New York: Putnam Juvenile.

Woodson, J. (2003). *Locomotion*. New York: Putnam. (Coretta Scott King Award Honor; National Book Award Finalist)

References

Alexander, P. A., Jetton, T., Kulikowich, J. M., & Woehler, C. A. (1994). Contrasting instructional and structural importance: The seductive effect of teacher questions. *Journal of Reading Behavior, 26,* 19–45.

Armbruster, B. B., Anderson, T. H., & Ostertag, J. (1987). Does text structure/summarization instruction facilitate learning from expository text? *Reading Research Quarterly, 22*(3), 331–346.

Baker, L., & Wigfield, A. (1999). Dimensions of children's motivation for reading and their relations to reading activity and reading achievement. *Reading Research Quarterly, 34*(4), 452–477.

Baumann, J. F., Edwards, E. C., Font, G., Tereshinski, C. A., Kame'enui, E. J., & Olejnik, S. (2002). Teaching morphemic and contextual analysis to fifth-grade students. *Reading Research Quarterly, 37*(2), 150–176.

Bean, T. W., & Steenwyk, F. L. (1984). The effect of three forms of summarization instruction on sixth graders' summary writing and comprehension. *Journal of Reading Behavior, 16*(4), 297–306.

Beck, I., McKeown, M., & Kucan, L. (2002). *Bringing words to life: Robust vocabulary instruction.* New York: Guilford Press.

Beck, I., McKeown, M., & Kucan, L. (2008). *Creating robust vocabulary: Frequently asked questions and extended examples.* New York: Guilford Press.

Beck, I., Omanson, R. C., & McKeown, M. G. (1982). An instructional redesign of reading lessons: Effects on comprehension. *Reading Research Quarterly, 17*(4), 462–481.

Blachowicz, C., & Fisher, P. (2002). *Teaching vocabulary in all classrooms.* Upper Saddle River, NJ: Merrill/Prentice Hall.

Blachowicz, C., & Ogle, D. (2008). *Reading comprehension: Strategies for independent learners* (2nd ed.). New York: Guilford Press.

Boyd, M. P., & Galda, L. (2011). *Real talk in elementary classrooms: Effective oral language practice.* New York: Guilford Press.

Bromley, K. (2011). Building a sound writing program. In L. B. Gambrell, L. M. Morrow, S. B. Neuman, & M. Pressley (Eds.), *Best practices in literacy instruction* (4th ed., pp. 295–318). New York: Guilford Press.

Brown, A. L., & Day, J. D. (1983). Macrorules for summarizing text: The development of expertise. *Journal of Verbal Learning and Verbal Behavior, 22,* 1–14.

Cain, K., & Oakhill, J. (2007). Reading comprehension difficulties: Correlates, causes, and consequences. In K. Cain & J. Oakhill (Eds.), *Children's comprehension problems in oral and written language* (pp. 41–75). New York: Guilford Press.

Calkins, L. M. (1994). *The art of teaching writing.* Portsmouth, NH: Heinemann.

Calkins, L. M. (2003). *The nuts and bolts of teaching writing.* Portsmouth, NH: First Hand.

Calkins, L. M. (2006). *A guide to the writing workshop.* Portsmouth, NH: First Hand.

Casbergue, R. M., & Plauchê, M. B. (2005). Emergent writing: Classroom practices that support young writers' development. In R. Indrisano & J. R. Paratore (Eds.), *Learning to write, writing to learn: Theory and research in practice* (pp. 8–25). Newark, DE: International Reading Association.

Cazden, C. B. (1988). *Classroom discourse: The language of teaching and learning.* Portsmouth, NH: Heinemann.

Cazden, C. B. (2001). *Classroom discourse: The language of teaching and learning.* Portsmouth, NH: Heinemann.

Coleman, D., & Pimentel, S. (2012). Revised publishers' criteria for the Common Core State Standards in English language arts and literacy, grades 3–12. Retrieved September 20, 2012, from *www.corestandards.org/assets/Publishers_Criteria_for_3–12.pdf.*

Denton, P. (2007). *The power of our words: Teacher language that helps children learn.* Turners Falls, MA: Northeast Foundation for Children.

Dole, J. A., Brown, K. J., & Trathen, W. (1996). The effects of strategy instruction on the comprehension performance of at-risk students. *Reading Research Quarterly, 31*(1), 62–88. Retrieved from *www.jstor.org/stable/748240.*

Dole, J. A., Duffy, G. G., Roehler, L. R., & Pearson, P. D. (1991). Moving from the old to the new: Research on reading comprehension instruction. *Review of Educational Research, 61*(2), 239–264.

Donovan, C. A., & Smolkin, L. B. (2006). Children's understanding of genre and writing development. In C. A. MacArthur, S. Graham, & J. Fitzgerald (Eds.), *Handbook of writing research* (pp. 131–143). New York: Guilford Press.

Duffy, G. G. (2009). *Explaining reading: A resource for teaching concepts, skills, and strategies* (2nd ed.). New York: Guilford Press.

Duffy, G. G., Roehler, L., Sivan, E., Rackliffe, G., Book, C., Meloth, M. S., et al. (1987). Effects of explaining the reasoning associated with using reading strategies. *Reading Research Quarterly, 22*(3), 347–368.

Duke, N. K., & Pearson, P. D. (2002). Effective practices for developing reading comprehension. In A. E. Farstrup & S. J. Samuels (Eds.), *What research has to say about reading instruction* (3rd ed., pp. 205–242). Newark, DE: International Reading Association.

Dyson, A. H., & Freedman, S. W. (1991). Writing. In J. Jenson, J. Flood, D. Lapp, & J. Squire (Eds.), *Handbook of research on teaching the English language arts* (pp. 754–774). New York: Macmillan.

Elbow, P. (1973). *Writing without teachers.* Oxford, UK: Oxford University Press.

Fisher, D., Frey, N., & Lapp, D. (2009). *In a reading state of mind: Brain research, teacher modeling, and comprehension instruction.* Newark, DE: International Reading Association.

Ford-Connors, E. (2011). Examining middle school teachers' talk during vocabulary instruction. *Yearbook of the Literacy Research Association, 60,* 229–244.

Frey, N., & Fisher, D. (2010). Identifying instructional moves during guided learning. *The Reading Teacher, 64*(2), 84–95.

Fukkink, R. G., & de Glopper, K. (1998). Effects of instruction in deriving meaning from context: A meta-analysis. *Review of Educational Research, 68*(4), 450–469.

Gaskins, I. W., Anderson, R. C., Pressley, M., Cunicelli, E. A., & Saltow, E. (1993). Six teachers' dialogue during cognitive process instruction. *Elementary School Journal, 93*(3), 277–304.

Glynn, S. M., Britton, B., Muth, D., & Dogan, N. (1982). Writing and revising persuasive documents: Cognitive demands. *Journal of Educational Psychology, 74,* 557–567.

Goodman, Y. (1978). Kid-watching: An alternative to testing. *National Elementary Principal, 57*(4), 41–45.

Graham, S., & Harris, K. R. (2007). Best practices in teaching planning. In S. Graham, C. A. MacArthur, & J. Fitzgerald (Eds.), *Best practices in writing instruction* (pp. 119–140). New York: Guilford Press.

Graham, S., & Harris, K. R. (2011). Writing difficulties. In A. McGill-Franzen & R. L. Allington (Eds.), *Handbook of reading disability research* (pp. 232–241). New York: Routledge.

Graham, S., & Perin, D. (2007). A meta-analysis of writing instruction for adolescent students. *Journal of Educational Psychology, 99*(3), 445–476.

Graves, D. H. (1983). *Writing: Teachers and children at work.* Portsmouth, NH: Heinemann.

Graves, M. F. (2009). *Essential readings on vocabulary instruction.* Newark, DE: International Reading Association.

Graves, M. F., Juel, C., Graves, B. B., & Dewitz, P. (2011). *Teaching reading in the 21st century: Motivating all learners.* Boston: Pearson Education.

Graves, M., & Watts-Taffe, S. M. (2002). The place of word conciousness in a research-based vocabulary program. In A. Farstrup & J. Samuels (Eds.), *What research has to say about reading instruction* (pp. 140–165). Newark, DE: International Reading Association.

Guthrie, J. T., & Humenick, N. M. (2004). Motivating students to read: Evidence for classroom practices that increase reading motivation and achievement. In P. McCardle & V. Chhabra (Eds.), *The voice of evidence in reading research* (pp. 329–354). Baltimore: Brookes.

Hansen, J. (1981). The effects of inference training and practice on young children's reading comprehension. *Reading Research Quarterly, 16*(3), 319–417.

Hansen, J., & Graves, D. H. (1991). Unifying the language arts curriculum: The language arts interact. In J. Jenson, J. Flood, D. Lapp, & J. Squire (Eds.), *Handbook of research on teaching the English language arts* (pp. 805–819). New York: Macmillan.

Jetton, T. L., & Alexander, P. A. (1997). Instructional importance: What teachers value and what students learn. *Reading Research Quarterly, 32*(3), 290–308.

Jiménez, R. T., García, G. E., & Pearson, P. D. (1995). Three children, two languages, and strategic reading: Case studies in bilingual/monolingual reading. *American Educational Research Journal, 32*(1), 67–97.

Johnston, P. H. (2004). *Choice words: How our language affects children's learning.* Portland, ME: Stenhouse.

Johnston, P. H. (2012). *Opening minds: Using language to chance lives.* Portland, ME: Stenhouse.

Johnston, P. H., Ivey, G., & Faulkner, A. (2011). Talking in class: Remembering what is important about classroom talk. *The Reading Teacher, 65*(4), 232–237.

Kamberelis, G. (1998). Relationships between children's literacy diets and genre development: You write what you read. *Literacy Teaching and Learning, 3,* 7–53.

Lipson, M. Y., & Wixson, K. K. (2009). *Assessment and instruction of reading and writing difficulty: An interactive approach* (4th ed.). Carlton, MA: Allyn & Bacon.

MacArthur, C. A., & Graham, S. (1987). Learning disabled students' composing with three methods: Handwriting, dictation, and word processing. *Journal of Special Education, 21,* 22–42.

McGee, L. (1982). Awareness of text structure: Effects on children's recall of expository text. *Reading Research Quarterly, 17,* 581–590.

McNeil, J., & Donant, L. (1982). Summarization strategy for improving reading comprehension. In J. A. Niles & L. A. Harris (Eds.), *New inquiries in reading research and instruction* (pp. 215–219). Rochester, NY: National Reading Conference.

Mercer, N., Wgerif, R., & Dawes, L. (1999). Children's talk and the development of reasoning in the classroom. *British Educational Research Journal, 25*(1), 95–111.

Nagy, W. E., & Anderson, R. C. (1984). How many words are there in printed school English? *Reading Research Quarterly, 19,* 303–330.

Nagy, W. E., Anderson, R. C., & Herman, P. A. (1987). Learning word meanings from context during normal reading. *American Educational Research Journal, 24*(2), 237–270.

Nagy, W. E., Berninger, V. W., & Abbott, R. D. (2006). Contributions of morphology beyond phonology to literacy outcomes of upper elementary and middle-school students. *Journal of Educational Psychology, 98*(1), 134–147.

Nagy, W. E., & Scott, J. A. (2000). Vocabulary processes. In M. L. Kamil, P. B. Mosenthal, P. D. Pearson, & R. Barr (Eds.), *Handbook of reading research* (pp. 269–284). Mahwah, NJ: Erlbaum.

National Governors Association Center for Best Practices and Council of Chief State School Officers. (2010). *Common Core State Standards initiative coordinated by National Governors Association Center for Best Practices and Council of Chief State School Officers.* Retrieved July 11, 2012, from *www.corestandards.org.*

Newkirk, T. (2010). The case for slow reading. *Educational Leadership, 67*(6), 6–11.

Paris, S. G., Lipson, M. Y., & Wixson, K. K. (1994). Becoming a strategic reader. In R. B. Ruddell, M. R. Ruddell, & H. Singer (Eds.), *Theoretical models and processes of reading* (4th ed., pp. 788–810). Newark, DE: International Reading Association.

Pressley, M. (2006, April). *What the future of reading research could be.* Paper presented at the International Reading Association's reading research conference, Chicago, IL.

Pressley, M., & Afflerbach, P. (1995). *Verbal protocols of reading: The nature of constructively responsive reading.* Hillsdale, NJ: Erlbaum.

Rasinski, T. V., Padak, N., Newton, J., & Newton, E. (2011). The Latin–Greek connection: Building vocabulary through morphological study. *The Reading Teacher, 65*(2), 133–141.

Reznitskaya, A. (2012). Dialogic teaching: Rethinking language use during literature discussions. *The Reading Teacher, 65*(7), 446–456.

Roser, N. L., & Bomer, K. (2005). Writing in primary classrooms: A teacher's story. In R. Indrisano & J. R. Paratore (Eds.), *Learning to write, writing to learn: Theory and research in practice* (pp. 26–39). Newark, DE: International Reading Association.

Schwanenflugel, P., Stahl, S. A., & McFalls, E. (1997). Partial word knowledge and vocabulary growth during reading comprehension. *Journal of Literacy Research, 29*(4), 531–553.

Shanahan, T., Callison, K., Carriere, C., Duke, N. K., Pearson, P. D., Schatschneider, C., et al. (2010). *Improving reading comprehension in kindergarten through 3rd grade: A practice guide* (NCEE 2010-4038). Washington, DC: National Center for Education Evaluation and Regional Assistance, Institute of Education Sciences, U.S. Department of Education. Retrieved from *http://whatworks.ed.gov/publications/practiceguides.*

Stahl, S. A., & Fairbanks, M. M. (1986). The effects of vocabulary instruction: A model based meta-analysis. *Review of Educational Research, 56*(1), 72–110.

Swanborn, M., & de Glopper, K. (1999). Incidental word learning while reading: A meta-analysis. *Review of Educational Research, 69*(3), 261–285.

Tierney, R. J., & Cunningham, J. W. (1984). Research on teaching reading comprehension. In P. D. Pearson, R. Barr, M. Kamil, & P. Mosenthal (Eds.), *Handbook of reading research* (Vol. 1, pp. 609–655). New York: Longman.

Wells, G. (1993). Reevaluating the IRE sequence: A proposal for the articulation of theories of activity and discourse for analysis of teaching and learning in the classroom. *Linguistics and Education, 5*, 1–37.

Wells, G. (2001). The case for dialogic inquiry. In G. Wells (Ed.), *Action, talk, and text* (pp. 171–194). New York: Teachers College Press.

Wiggins, G. (1993). *Assessing student performance: Understanding the purpose and limits of testing.* San Francisco: Jossey-Bass.

Wolf, M. K., Crosson, A. C., & Resnick, L. B. (2006). *Accountable talk in reading comprehension instruction.* CSE Technical Report 670. Los Angeles: National Center for Research on Evaluation, Standards, and Student Testing.

Children's Literature

Abrahams, P. (2005). *Down the rabbit hole.* New York: HarperCollins.

Bunting, E. (1993). *Fly away home.* New York: Clarion Books.

Cooney, C. B. (2005). *Code orange.* New York: Random House.

DiCamillo, K. (2006). *The miraculous journey of Edward Tulane.* Cambridge, MA: Candlewick Press.

DiCamillo, K. (2009). *Mercy Watson goes for a ride.* Cambridge, MA: Candlewick Press.

Estes, E. (1973). *The hundred dresses.* New York: Scholastic.

Hartland, J. (2007). *Night shift.* New York: Bloomsbury USA.

Jenner, C. (2008). *Welcome to China.* New York: DK Publishing.

Kalman, B. (2004). *Endangered tigers.* New York: Crabtree Publishing.

National Geographic Reading Expeditions. *Pennsylvania. www.ngschoolpub.com.*

Orloff, K. K. (2004). *I wanna iguana.* New York: Putnam.

Perkins, M. (2004). *Monsoon summer.* New York: Delacorte Press.

Ray, M. L. (2001). *Mud.* New York: First Voyager Books.

Sachar, L. (1998). *Holes.* New York: Dell Yearling.

Sebag-Montefiore, H. (2007). *China.* New York: DK Publishing.

Spinelli, J. (2000). *Stargirl.* New York: Dell Laurel-Leaf.

Steig, W. (1971). *Amos and Boris.* New York: Farrar, Straus & Giroux.

Tebow, T., & Whitaker, N. (2011). *Through my eyes.* New York: Harper.

Index